# LIVE LIKE A CATHOLIC

A Study of the Interior Castle by St. Teresa of Avila

By

Susan Brinkmann, OCDS

PO Box 1173
Pottstown, PA 19464

**NIHIL OBSTAT:**
Robert A. Pesarchick, STD, STL, MA, M.Div

**IMPRIMATUR:**
Archbishop Charles J. Chaput, OFM Cap.
No. 00512, March 10, 2015



**Catholic Life Institutes Press**
**PO Box 1173**
**Pottstown, PA 19464**
**www.catholiclifeinstitute.org**

Interior Design and Layout by ElizabethRacine.com

Cover Design by IGD Graphic Design, www.image-gd.com

**Live Like a Catholic/ Susan Brinkmann**. -- 1st ed.
ISBN 978-1-7336724-0-5

*"Let us now imagine that this castle . . . contains many mansions, some above, others below, others at each side; and in the center and midst of them all is the chiefest mansion where the most secret things pass between God and the soul."*

*St. Teresa of Avila*

# CONTENTS

There's a kingdom inside you, a magnificent castle filled with mystical delights and supernatural adventures. This interior castle is the domain of those willing to let go of the worldly in order to grasp the other-worldly. They cling to nothing except Him who said, ". . . the kingdom of God is within you."[1]

What is this kingdom and where can we find it?

This question was once asked by St. Teresa of Avila, the great mystical doctor of the Church who lived 500 years ago. While deep in prayer, she wondered what the soul looked like and the Lord favored her with a most remarkable intellectual vision.

"I began to think to the soul as if it were a castle made of a single diamond," the saint wrote, "or of very clear crystal, in which there are many rooms, just as in Heaven there are many mansions."[2]

Some mansions were above, others below, others at each side. "And in the center and midst of them all is the

---

[1] Luke 17:21 (*Douay Rheims*)

[2] Avila, Teresa, *Interior Castle*, translated and edited by E. Allison Peers (New York, NY, *Doubleday Books*, 1989), pg. 28

chiefest mansion where the most secret things pass between God and the soul."[3]

The central mansion issued a brilliant light that penetrated into the outermost mansions of the castle. The further away from the center, the dimmer the light. Teresa was made to understand that the whole goal of a person's life was to penetrate that central mansion where they would achieve what is known as the transforming union - or spiritual marriage - with God. This union is the height of one's mystical experience on earth. Beyond this, there is nothing left but the Beatific Vision.

When St. Teresa told her confessor about the vision, he asked her to write it down. She scoffed, "Let the learned men do the writing and leave me to my spinning."

But she obeyed and sat down to do as he asked. She was still wondering what on earth to write when she picked up her pen and put to paper what would become one of the greatest works of mystical theology in existence today - the *Interior Castle*.

Contained in this one volume is the entire course of the mystical life from conversion to transforming union. It also contains a veritable encyclopedia on Catholic prayer, describing the four primary stages from beginner or "first stage" to the "fourth stage" with its accompanying ecstatic union with God. Even more important, the *Interior Castle* clearly explains how

---

[3] *Interior Castle*, pg. 29

growth in the spiritual life dramatically affects our prayer life.

But why do we need to know about our spiritual development? Doesn't "wondering where we are" in our spiritual life shift our attention from God to ourselves?

Yes, but while it is true that we should not be introspective while pursuing the interior life, it is also true that the person who lacks a practical understanding of the stages of prayer and the mystical life places themselves at a distinct disadvantage, especially when hardships come.

For instance, the person who doesn't understand that progress in prayer often means long dry spells devoid of all consolation can easily turn away from the true path and become a kind of religious "thrill seeker", gladly pursuing all those trendy New Age styles of mind-blanking prayer and a preoccupation with the self rather than the Divine.

A lack of knowledge about the ways of the interior life also leaves us unprepared for advances in prayer that go far beyond the realm of vocal prayer. Because we don't know any better, we assume that mystical forms of prayer, such as infused contemplation, are meant only for those in cloistered orders. We have no way of knowing that God gives to whom He wills, what He wills, when He wills - which pretty much includes everybody.

But if we don't know where we're going, the unenlightened soul may actually flee in fear from advanced favors from God because they don't understand what's happening to them.

St. Teresa writes: "If the Lord grants you these favors, it will be a great consolation to you to know that such things are possible . . . Sometimes He will do this only to manifest His power, as He said to the blind man to whom He gave his sight . . . He grants these favors not because those who receive them are holier than those who do not, but in order that His greatness may be made known . . ."[4]

What kind of favors is she talking about? As those of you know who took the first course in this series, *Pray Like a Catholic*, experiences such as ecstasies, raptures, wounds of love as well as transports and flights of spirit are all considered common by theologians.

Yes, common - even to us ordinary folk.

Many of us don't think this is possible because they have yet to discover the God in whose image we were made. Until we do, we'll never really know who we are or what we're capable of achieving in the spiritual life.

## What is the Soul?

---

[4] *Interior Castle*, pg. 30

In order to better comprehend the kind of journey we are about to undertake, we must first come to understand the human soul. What is it? And how can it be that the Lord actually dwells within us?

If you can't answer any of those questions, don't feel bad. Mankind has been struggling to make sense out of what we call the soul since antiquity. Some believe it is a kind of life-force energy; other say it's a mysterious object hidden in an untapped corner of the brain.

The *Catechism* teaches us to find our answers in Sacred Scripture where the term 'soul' often refers to human *life* or the entire human *person*. The "soul" also refers to "the innermost aspect of man, that which is of greatest value in him, that by which he is most especially in God's image."[5]

However, the human body also shares in the dignity of the image of God. "It is a human body precisely because it is animated by a spiritual soul and it is the whole human person that is intended to become, in the body of Christ, a temple of the Spirit. Man, though made of body and soul, is a unity."[6]

It's interesting to note that because we are created in God's image - and He has both male and female qualities - that our souls are thought to have the same gender as our bodies. Therefore, we are male or female in soul as well as body.

---

[5] *Catechism of the Catholic Church* (New York, NY; *Catholic Book Publishing Company,* 1994) No. 363
[6] Ibid. No. 364

"Sexuality affects all aspects of the human person in the unity of his body and soul."[7]

Elaborating on this teaching, Dr. Peter Kreeft writes that "Our sexual identity extends to our souls, our personalities, our spirits. There is indeed a 'feminine mind' and a 'masculine mind' as well as body, for we are a psychosomatic unity (soul-body unity). To think of one's soul as neither masculine nor feminine is to separate body and soul artificially, as did the ancient Gnostics, and to think of the soul as a sexless 'ghost in the machine' instead of as the life and form *of the body*, and to think of masculinity and femininity as merely a material, animal thing."[8]

Catholics believe that every spiritual soul is created immediately by God and is not produced by the parents.[9]

We also believe that the soul is immortal. "It does not perish when it separates from the body at death, and it will be reunited with the body at the final Resurrection."[10]

As Dr. Richard Geraghty explains for *EWTN*, the soul is a spiritual or immaterial thing which means it has no physical parts that can fall apart, get sick, be crushed, or otherwise put out of existence. This is how we know that it will live forever.

---

[7] *Catechism*, No. 2332
[8] Dr. Peter Kreeft, *Catholic Christianity* (San Francisco: *Ignatius Press*, 2001), 244
[9] Ibid, No. 365
[10] Ibid, No. 366

"For this reason the souls of the saved will always be aware of themselves as enjoying the vision of God for all eternity. This enjoyment will be the result of having chosen to act on earth in such a way that one did the will of God rather than one's own will. And the souls of the damned will be aware of themselves as never attaining this vision of God because they have shown by their lives on earth that they did not wish this vision but instead preferred their own will."[11]

Some people also wonder if the soul is the same thing as the spirit of a person.

Yes, but as the *Catechism* explains, sometimes the soul is distinguished from the spirit, such as when St. Paul prays that God will sanctify His people "wholly", with "spirit and soul and body".[12]

"The Church teaches that this distinction does not introduce a duality into the soul. Spirit signifies that from creation man is ordered to a supernatural end and that his soul can gratuitously be raised beyond all it deserves to communion with God."[13]

In other words, the soul is not comprised of two parts - a "spirit" and a "soul".

---

[11] Geraghty, Richard, Ph.D. Pets in Heaven? (Accessed at *EWTN*, 12/27/13 http://www.ewtn.com/expert/answers/pets_in_heaven.htm)
[12] 1 Thess 5:23
[13] *Catechism*, No. 367

However some spiritual writers such as St. Francis de Sales use the terms to distinguish between the upper or summit of the soul (spirit) from its lower part (soul).

This is the view of the great Dominican theologian Father Reginald Garrigou-Lagrange who says the soul has different regions within it.

The region belonging to the sensible order as opposed to the suprasensible or intellectual order, is common to men and animals.

" . . . ( I)t includes the external senses and the internal senses, comprising the imagination, the sensible memory, and also sensibility, or the sensitive appetite, whence spring the various passions or emotions which we call sensible love and hatred, desire and aversion, sensible joy and sadness, hope and despair, audacity and fear, and anger. All this sensitive life exists in the animal, whether its passions are mild like those of the dove or lamb, or whether they are strong like those of the wolf and the lion."[14]

Residing "above" this sensitive part is the intellectual part which is common to men and angels, although it is far more vigorous and beautiful in the angel, Lagrange states. The intellectual part of the soul towers above the body, which is why we say the soul is spiritual and does not depend on the body for its existence, thus allowing it to survive the body after death.

---

[14] Garrigou-Lagrange, Reginald, O.P., *The Three Ages of the Interior Life* (Rockford, Ill.; *Tan Books and Publishers*, 1989) pg. 48-49

"From the essence of the soul in this elevated region spring our two higher faculties, the intellect and the will," he states. "The intellect knows not only sensible qualities, colors and sounds, but also being, the intelligible reality of necessary and universal truths" such as the difference between right and wrong. An animal will never attain to the knowledge of these principles.

"Since the intellect knows the good in a universal manner, and not only the delectable or useful good but the upright and reasonable good (for example: Die rather than become a traitor), it follows that the will can love this good, will it, and accomplish it. Thereby the intellect immensely dominates the sensitive part or the emotions common to men and animals. By his intellect and his will, man resembles the angel . . ."[15]

We all know that some people can develop these two higher faculties of intellect and will and become people of genius, and they can do so without developing a loving and intimate life with God, which is "of another order," Lagrange states. This other order is entirely supernatural and applies to both man and angel.

"Man and angel can indeed know God naturally from without, by the reflection of His perfections in creatures; but no created and creatable intellect can by its natural powers attain, even confusedly and obscurely, the essential and formal object of the divine intellect."

---

[15] *The Three Ages of the Interior Life*, pg. 49-50

For this higher form of intellect to function, we need sanctifying grace which introduces us into a higher order of truth and life.

This is what Saint Paul means when he says that "For what man knows the things of a man, but the spirit of a man that is in him? So the things also that are of God no man knows, but the Spirit of God"[16]

We receive this grace at our baptism and thus begin to live this higher, supra-angelic order of the intimate life with God.

Lagrange describes this grace, which we receive at baptism, as a "divine graft" that is received in the very essence of the soul "to elevate its vitality and to make it bear no longer merely natural fruits but supernatural ones, meritorious acts that merit eternal life for us."

With it, we begin to live this higher, supra-angelic order of life with God which he describes as "immensely superior to a sensible miracle . . . ."[17]

As we will learn during the course of our journey into the "interior castle" known as our soul, this life of grace develops in us under the form of the infused virtues and the seven gifts of the Holy Spirit - which is why each chapter will highlight the virtue most vital to that stage in the journey.

But how is it that God can "dwell" within our souls?

---

[16] 1 Cor. 2:11

[17] *The Three Ages of the Interior Life*, pg. 50-51

This miraculous indwelling occurs at the moment of our baptism when the Holy Spirit - and along with Him the Father and the Son - takes up His abode within our souls. Jesus announced this when he said "If anyone love me . . . my Father will love him, and we will come to him, and will make our abode with him."[18]

"These words reveal to us the mystery of the indwelling of the Trinity in our souls, an indwelling which implies a very special presence of God within us," writes Father Gabriel of St. Mary Magdalen. "If we are in a state of grace, God not only dwells in us, but since He is the living God, He lives in us; He lives His intimate life, the life of the Trinity." [19]

God gives Himself to us now just as He once willed to give Himself to Adam and Eve who were created in the state of grace and enjoyed this intimacy of life with God. They lost this gift when they fell from grace, but it was restored after Jesus' death when the Father sent the promised "Paraclete" to once again enable man to live in this special intimate union with his Creator.

However, even though the soul needs only a single degree of grace in order to live in intimacy with the Trinity, this intimacy has different degrees.

"It becomes closer and more profound according as the soul, growing in grace and charity, acquires a greater

---

[18] John 14:23

[19] Gabriel, Father, of St. Mary Magdalen, *Divine Intimacy* (Rockford, Ill., *Tan Books and Publishers*) 1996, pg 663

capacity for entering into a deeper relationship with the Blessed Trinity," Father Gabriel explains.

It's much like two persons who are friends and who live in the same house. As their mutual affection for one another increases, their friendship becomes more intense and even though they were already present to one another, this presence takes on a whole new aspect as they grow closer and closer.

In much the same way, even though the Trinity already inhabits our soul today, their Presence can always be made stronger in terms of a more intimate relationship with us as we progress in the spiritual life and acquire additional degrees of grace by advancing in charity.

But it's important to understand that even though this progress can produce new effects in our soul, sometimes referred to as "new visits" of the Divine Persons, in reality, they're always present in our souls.

"Their visit does not come from without but from within the soul itself, where they dwell," Fr. Gabriel explains.

Just like our illustration of the two friends, they're always together, but that togetherness is becoming more intense, more meaningful, as their friendship deepens.

Jesus' promise that "If anyone love Me . . . We will come to him and will make our abode with him" is never exhausted, Father explains.

"It is always new, always ready to be actualized every time the conditions for it are renewed, that is, every time we love more intensely."

This should spur us on to strive for constant progress in love because the Blessed Trinity "will set no limits to the effusion of charity and grace in our soul, provided we place no obstacle to their development."[20]

These obstacles, which will be referred to as "Roadblocks" during this study, come in many forms, from clinging to sinful habits and lack of trust in God to resisting a deeper commitment to the Gospel and a fear of what others will think of us.

Perhaps now it is easier to understand why Teresa of Avila felt only pity for those who live their lives on the material surface rather than on that immensely higher plane of potential union with God.

"It is no small pity, and should cause no little shame, that, through our own fault, we don't not understand ourselves or know who we are," St. Teresa writes. "As to what good qualities there may be in our souls, or Who dwells within them, or how precious they are, those are things we seldom consider and so we trouble little about carefully preserving the soul's beauty."[21]

---

[20] *Divine Intimacy*, pg. 667

[21] Ibid, pg. 29

For most of us, the focus of our life is almost entirely on our bodies rather than on our souls. In St. Teresa's estimation, this is the equivalent of admiring the setting rather than the diamond.

In the course of this study, we will learn to look beyond the setting, and see the diamond within us - the precious God who dwells in the very center of our soul, and who is longing to unite us with Himself in an eternal union of love.

## *For Reflection*

1. Considering the overview of the seven mansions and four stages of prayer that you have received thus far, what emotions does the idea of this kind of interior journey invoke within you? Fear? Excitement? Intrigue?

______________________________________________

______________________________________________

______________________________________________

______________________________________________

______________________________________________

______________________

2. Theologians explain that man most resembles the angel in the upper part of our soul - the intellect and the will. Since the intellect knows the good in a universal manner, it follows that the will can love this good, will it, and accomplish it. What are examples in your daily life when you are using the powers of the upper region of the soul and when are you exercising the lower region of the soul?

3. We know that if we are in a state of grace, God not only dwells in us, but also lives in us. When are you the most aware of this Presence in your daily life?

4. Even though the soul needs only a single degree of grace in order to live in intimacy with the Trinity, this intimacy grows according to our growth in charity. What are some ways that you can grow in charity in your daily life? Are there areas where you are harboring resentments or lack of forgiveness that are impeding your growth in charity? Are you too concerned with yourself and your own interests to be as available to others as you ought to be? What steps can you take to begin to tear down these barriers to growth?

________________________________________

________________________________________

________________________________________

________________________________________

________________________________________

________________________________________

________________________________________

________________________________________

CHAPTER ONE

# THE FIRST MANSION

The door leading into this splendid "castle" we call the soul cannot be opened by good works or fine intentions. Only one key fits this lock - prayer.

When a person first enters this castle, they are usually coming from a very worldly lifestyle and are still overly preoccupied with temporal affairs. Perhaps they suffered some kind of misfortune in life, an illness or other calamity, or maybe they just came to the realization that there has to be more to life than stockpiling wealth. Whatever the case, something made them turn to God and pray in a genuine way. It might have been a cry for help, or just a moan of dismay, but it was for real - and it opened a door.

We have now entered the outermost mansions, the rooms furthest away from the brilliant light contained in the seventh and most central room.

In her book, the *Interior Castle*, St. Teresa of Avila describes this place as being full of "many bad things -

snakes, vipers and poisonous creatures - which have come in with the soul . . ."[22]

These vile creatures represent the soul's constant concern with worldly affairs, possessions, honors. The brilliant light radiating from the central mansion barely penetrates here and even if it did, the soul is too earthbound to enjoy it.

Even though they may not be in a state of mortal sin, they are so full of imperfections they can barely appreciate their newfound faith. "It is as if one were to enter a place flooded by sunlight but with eyes so full of dust that they can hardly open them," Teresa writes.

"This seems to me to be the condition of a soul which, though not in a bad state, is so completely absorbed in things of the world and so deeply immersed . . . in possession or honors or business, that, although . . . it would like to gaze at the castle and enjoy its beauty, it is prevented from doing so and seems quite unable to free itself from all these impediments."[23]

At this stage, the soul is its own worst enemy and is a slave to itself, to its passions, its unchristian-like behaviors, to casually committed venial sins and crab-like clinging to its possessions and ungodly companions.

---

[22] Avila, Teresa, *Interior Castle*, translated and edited by E. Allison Peers (New York, NY, *Doubleday Books*, 1989), pg. 40

[23] Ibid, pg. 41

However, they have one thing going for them, Teresa writes - their desires are good almost in spite of themselves.

"Sometimes . . . they think about their souls, though not very carefully. Full of a thousand preoccupations as they are, they pray only a few times a month, and as a rule, they are thinking all the time of their preoccupations, for they are very much attached to them. . .(W)here their treasure is, there is their heart also."[24]

For this reason, it's important for people in the first mansions to get to work cleaning all that "dust" out of their eyes. More than anything else, they must summon the courage to take a long hard look at themselves in a mirror called "self knowledge". Ultimately, we must confront the fact that there really is a God - and we aren't Him.

"Let us think of His greatness and then come back to our own baseness," St. Teresa suggests. "By looking at His purity, we shall see our foulness; by meditating on His humility, we shall see how far we are from being humble."

There's only one way to take this advice - we must learn how to pray.

---

[24] Interior Castle, pg. 32

## *Fuel for the Journey*

*Prayer*

The reason this is so important is because the only way to overcome our strong attraction to the pleasures of the world, which are so rooted in our nature, is to find a greater attraction, a higher love, that will lure us into letting go of these lesser loves.

As St. John of the Cross explains: "A love of pleasure and attachment to it, usually fires the will toward the enjoyment of things that give pleasure. A more intense enkindling of another, better love (love of the soul's Bridegroom) is necessary for the vanquishing of the appetites and the denial of this pleasure. By finding satisfaction and strength in this love, it will have the courage and constancy to readily deny all other appetites."[25]

We're not going to advance very far in our journey to God unless we know Who we're seeking and what makes Him so much more appealing than the things of earth. He is only too happy to teach us, but in order to do this, we must spend time with Him, get to know Him, to realize just how lovable He really is. This is what prayer is all about and why it will always be the most potent fuel we will use throughout our journey to the seventh mansion.

---

[25] John of the Cross, *The Ascent of Mount Carmel*, translated by Kieran Kavanaugh, OCD and Otilio Rodriquez, OCD (Washington DC, ICS Publications, 1991) pg. 151

What most beginners in the spiritual life don't realize is that there's a whole lot more to prayer than the rote prayers we learned in grade school. These stages of prayer occur naturally as we move through the mansions of the soul and grow in our faith. This is because prayer and growth in the spiritual life go hand-in-hand. We cannot have one without the other. If our commitment to Christ is deepening, so is our prayer, and vice versa.

Teresa of Avila describes four specific stages of prayer that the faithful soul can expect to travel through during the course of this journey. She uses the analogy of watering a garden to describe each stage.

In the first stage of prayer, we do most of the work, "watering our garden" with the use of a bucket and a great deal of human effort. This analogy represents the vocal/discursive prayer with which we all start - a type of prayer that requires much effort, especially because those who are in the early stages of the spiritual life are too worldly to keep their minds focused on spiritual matters. Their strong taste for worldly pleasures makes it difficult for them to concentrate on spiritual pleasures about which they are so unfamiliar and have so little taste. When they do manage to pray, it's mostly the recitation of vocal prayers and litanies.

Although vocal prayer will always be a part of our spiritual journey, in the beginning stages of the spiritual life, it is generally the only kind of prayer that the soul is capable of. This is why vocal/discursive prayer is generally associated with the first two mansions of the soul.

In the second stage of prayer, which often begins in the third mansions, God will start to do a little bit more of the work and will allow us to water our "garden" through the use of a water wheel, which requires less exertion on our part. We will have become more familiar with God by now, and have developed a real relationship with Him by persevering in our daily prayer. We have more of a taste for the spiritual realm and are filled with wonder when we contemplate God and all of His magnificent qualities. This makes it much easier to meditate and to take that very important step into mental prayer, which is nothing more than a loving one-on-one encounter with God. We begin to experience a wonderful contentment just being in the presence of God.

Another notable sign of this advancing stage of prayer is an increasing awareness of God dwelling within us - of His being present at all times. We find ourselves "talking" to Him or "sharing" the events of our day with Him outside the time normally set aside for prayer. St. Teresa teaches that developing this increasing awareness of the indwelling God is the best way to prepare ourselves for more advanced stages of prayer.

As the second stage of prayer moves closer to the third, we begin to experience the first taste of infused contemplation, which Father Thomas Dubay describes in his classic book, *Fire Within*, as an "infused and gentle awareness (of God) given by God and not produced by human effort. One is, as it were, gathered together in God and desires solitude to be alone with

Him. The senses and external things slowly lose their hold on the person. . . ."[26]

These first infusions are very delicate and brief and easily missed by the soul who is not well-versed in the ways of prayer. For instance, they may resist an "urge" to stop rattling off prayers and just sit quietly with God; or they may find themselves steeped in a deep and profound quiet and mistake this for wasting time or daydreaming.

Especially in these early experiences of infused prayer, "the beginner needs to be well instructed or he is likely to miss what is given at this point, so gentle and delicate it is," writes Fr. Dubay. "Being such, they can be easily stifled by unwise efforts to pray actively."[27]

As we progress into the fourth mansions, these absorptions in God become progressively more powerful. Called the Prayer of Quiet, God captures the will and unites it with His own, sometimes suspending the faculties so completely one is aware of nothing around them. Whole blocks of time (10-20 minutes) may sometimes disappear without one knowing or remembering anything about what took place. This is accompanied by a deep peace, not of human origin, that penetrates the soul and sometimes lingers for days afterward.

When we reach the third stage of prayer, which occurs in the fifth mansions, God is now doing most of

---

[26] Dubay, Thomas, S.M., *Fire Within* (San Francisco, CA, *Ignatius Press*, 1989) pg. 87

[27] Ibid, pg. 88

the work in prayer, "watering" our garden by means of a nearby stream or fountain. The profound silence of the Prayer of Quiet begins to give way to a much deeper absorption in God called the Prayer of Union or Spiritual Betrothal.

In this stage of prayer, not only is the will taken up by God, as was the case in the Prayer of Quiet, but also the imagination, memory and intellect. In the Prayer of Union, the person experiences a delight so deep and profound that St. Teresa of Avila describes the person as being "beside themselves" while experiencing it.

"The consolation, the sweetness, and the delight are incomparably greater than that experienced in the previous prayer. . . . This prayer is a glorious foolishness, a heavenly madness . . . . Often I had been as though bewildered and inebriated in this love . . . the soul would desire to cry out praises and is beside itself . . . it cannot bear so much joy . . ."[28]

The prayer of union is of a tender and more marital nature, which is why it is referred to as a "betrothal." The union takes place only in the interior of the soul and Teresa likens it to a "courtship" but one with "nothing that is not spiritual."

She explains that corporal union is different and that the spiritual joys and consolations given by the Lord "are a thousand leagues removed from those experienced in marriage. It is all a union of love with

[28] Teresa of Avila, *The Life of Teresa of Jesus*, Translated and Edited by E. Allison Peers, (Garden City, NY, *Image Books*, 1960) pg. 163

love, and its operations are entirely pure, and so delicate and gentle that there is no way of describing them."

In the fourth stage of prayer, which occurs in the sixth and seventh mansion, the garden of the soul is now being watered directly by God who is sending it a soft soaking rain from heaven. By this time, the soul has undergone two major stages of purification - the "night of the senses" and, much later, the "night of the soul." It has finally reached the summit of spiritual perfection and the purpose of its creation - the achievement of total union with God. The soul now lives for God alone, is well advanced in God-centeredness and in living the Gospel message.

Those who reach this level of prayer are so head-over-heels in love with God, it is painful for them to remain on earth. Sometimes the mere mention of the name of God is enough to send the soul into transports of joy. This is the stage where prayers of rapture, ecstasy and transports of spirit take place. These are experiences of deep union with God and are frequently accompanied by complete suspension of the faculties.

This is how St. Teresa once described a rapture. "Now when the body is in a rapture, it is as though dead, frequently unable to do anything of itself. It remains in the position it was when seized by the rapture, whether standing or sitting, with the hands open or closed . . . Even though it can't do anything of itself with regard to exterior things, it doesn't fail to understand and hear as though listening to something from far off."

God frequently soothes these souls with other forms of infused contemplation, such as transports of spirit where "The soul really seems to have left the body," St. Teresa writes. "On the other hand it is clear that the person is not dead. He feels as if he has been in another world . . .and has been shown a fresh light there, so unlike any to be found in this life that . . . it would be impossible for him to obtain any idea of it."[29]

When we enter the seventh mansion, the spiritual betrothal of the third stage of prayer, which takes place during the prayer of union, is now ready to advance to its final stage which is known as the prayer of transforming union or spiritual marriage.

According to St. Teresa of Avila, what the soul experiences during this marriage is beyond the scope of human language. In her case, it occurred just after she received communion one day and began when the Lord favored her with a vision unlike any other she had ever experienced.

"The Lord appeared in the center of the soul, not through an imaginary but through an intellectual vision, just as He appeared to the Apostles, without entering through the door . . . This instantaneous communication of God to the soul is so great a secret and so sublime a favor and such delight is felt by the soul that I do not know with what to compare it, beyond saying that the Lord is pleased to manifest to the soul . . . the glory that

---

[29] *Interior Castle,* pg. 160

is in heaven, in a more sublime manner than is possible through any vision or spiritual consolation."[30]

Nothing was seen with the eyes or the imagination, but was more like a sudden infusion of knowledge. It's as if God removes the "scales from the eyes of the soul" and allows it to "see" the Blessed Trinity.

Through a special kind of illumination, St. Tersea writes, the soul "sees these three Persons individually, and yet, with a wonderful kind of knowledge which is given to it, the soul realizes that . . . all these three Persons are one Substance, and one Power, and one Knowledge, and one God alone; so that what we hold by faith, the soul may be said here to grasp by sight, although nothing is seen by the eyes, either of the body or of the soul."[31]

After this mysterious union, the soul receives a whole new awareness of the indwelling Trinity. Unlike spiritual betrothal, when God and the soul would unite and then separate in the prayer of union, in spiritual marriage they become one on a permanent basis.

Teresa wrote that no matter how numerous were her trials and business worries, the essential part of her soul was permanently fixed in this placid dwelling place. She once described herself as feeling "divided" because her soul could remain in perfect peace even while life was erupting as usual all around her. Sometimes she would even grumble that her soul was "doing nothing but

---

[30] Ibid, pg. 213
[31] Ibid, pg. 209

enjoying itself" while she was left with all the trials of life.

This description should dismantle any notions that the person who reaches this stage of prayer does nothing but kneel in prayer and stare at the sky all day. Quite the contrary. These people are more alive than any of us.

"It would be a mistake to conclude that this person . . . is inert or living in a marginal manner," Father Dubay writes. "Inner life and vitality are increased . . . this is supreme living."[32]

By making this incredible journey into the heart of God, they have achieved the ultimate purpose in life and have become precisely the person they were created to be.

Now that you've had a glimpse of the incredible mystical journey we call "prayer," it's important to remember that infused prayer is a gift from God and can never be learned from a book or acquired through the mastering of techniques such as those taught in transcendental meditation and Centering Prayer. These and other forms of prayer that are based on eastern meditation techniques call for "blanking the mind" and trying to achieve that profound inner stillness by our own efforts. The most we will ever achieve is an altered state of consciousness, something that is not even remotely similar to the glorious experience of authentic immersion in the Triune God.

---

[32] *Fire Within*, pg. 98

In fact, Teresa of Avila says this herself when she explains that the silencing of the intellect is something only God can do. "Taking it upon oneself to stop and suspend thought is what I mean should not be done;' nor should we cease to work with the intellect, because otherwise we would be left like cold simpletons and be doing neither one thing nor the other. When the Lord suspends the intellect and causes it to stop, He Himself gives it that which holds its attention and makes it marvel; and without reflection it understands more in the space of a creed than we can understand with all our earthly diligence in many years. Trying to keep the soul's faculties busy and thinking you can make them be quiet is foolish."[33]

The kind of prayer that will accompany our journey through the mansions is something that is wholly "received" and no amount of effort on our part can "make it happen."

Instead of trying to experience "spiritual highs", the person in the first mansion has much more important work to be done if he or she wishes to advance to the next mansion.

Specifically, this person needs to get to work on cleaning up their distorted way of looking at the world.

---

[33] Avila, Teresa, *Way of Perfection* (chapter 31, pg 209)

## ***Roadblock***

*A Distorted Worldview*

At this early stage in our spiritual awakening, we are living in a very small and contracted world, one which includes only the material - our possessions and the people who inhabit our life. Our highest ideals are to achieve a bigger paycheck, buy a bigger home, wear the latest fashions and drive the most expensive car. We are so engrossed in ourselves and our own little world that we fail to see the bigger picture of life - who we are, why we're here, where we're going.

This is why Teresa is so adamant that those who reside in the first mansion need to focus on acquiring authentic self-knowledge - which begins by discovering who we really are and where we belong in the overall scheme of things.

"It is absurd to think that we can enter Heaven without first entering our own souls - without getting to know ourselves, and reflecting upon the wretchedness of our nature and what we owe to God, and continually imploring His mercy."[34]

We start this process by getting to know ourselves in the eyes of God, something that begins to occur when we take up the habit of prayer. The Person we encounter in prayer seems to know us in a very deep and profound way, seemingly from the inside out. It becomes more

---

[34] *Interior Castle*, pg. 53

and more obvious that He is, in fact, our Creator, and it was He who willed us into being.

This is a crucial step in our quest for self-knowledge because no one can know who they are unless they first learn where they came from.

"It is no small pity, and should cause us no little shame that, through our own fault, we do not understand ourselves or know who we are," Teresa laments.

"Would it not be a sign of great ignorance, my daughters, if a person were asked who he was and could not say, and had no idea who his father or his mother was, or from what country he came? Though that is great stupidity, our own is incomparably greater if we make no attempt to discover what we are, and only know that we are living in these bodies, and have a vague idea, because we have heard it and because our Faith tells us so, that we possess souls. As to what good qualities there may be in our souls, or Who dwells within them, or how precious they are - those are things which we seldom consider and so we trouble little about carefully preserving the soul's beauty. All our interest is centered in the rough setting of the diamond, and in the outer wall of the castle - that is to say, in these bodies of ours."[35]

Realizing that we are sons and daughters of God changes everything - especially our worldview.

---

[35] *Interior Castle*, pg. 29

For starters, we're no longer the center of our universe. That years-long build-up of pride that left us living in a self-centered and selfish world gives way to a new humility.

"Humility makes us realize that, in the sight of God, we are only His little creature, entirely dependent upon Him for our existence and for all our works," writes Father Gabriel of St. Mary Magdalen.

"Having received life from God, we cannot subsist even one moment independently of Him. He who gave us existence by His creative action, maintains life in us by His conserving action. . . . It follows that everything we possess in the order of being - qualities, gifts, capacities - and everything we have accomplished in the order of action, is not ours, but all, in one way or another, are gifts of God, all are acts performed with God's help."[36]

We suddenly understand what St. Paul meant when he asked the people, "What do you possess that you have not received? But if you have received it, why are you boasting as if you did not receive it?"[37]

To the spiritual neophyte, these truths are humbling, even shocking at first, but it is the only way to realize what Jesus meant when He said, " . . . without me you can do nothing." [38]

---

[36] Gabriel, Father of Mary Magdalen, OCD, *Divine Intimacy* (Rockford, Ill., *Tan Books & Publishers*, 1996) pg 315-315

[37] 1 Cor. 4:7

[38] John 15:5

If we are to get anywhere in the spiritual life, it will be by grace alone. And in order to acquire grace, we must ask for it, which is why we must pray every day without fail.

As these truths begin to sink in and take root within our souls, we naturally begin to develop a genuine fear of the Lord.

"The biblical fear of the Lord is an intelligent fear, based on a deep perception of the holiness and majesty of God, which right recognizes the possibility of violating the law of God, despising His love, rejecting His mercy, and meriting eternal separation from Him," writes Ralph Martin.[39]

This is why Scripture tells us that "the fear of the Lord is the beginning of wisdom . . ."[40]

This wisdom, which we receive through the Holy Spirit's gift of Wisdom, is like receiving a higher form of intelligence, or a kind of radar vision that is able to see through the deceptive rhetoric of the world. For instance, we're no longer deceived by calls for "personal choice" and "tolerance" when they really mean providing cover for a variety of social sins. We can suddenly see through it all, and this too, is very humbling - especially when it leads us to a real examination of our own conscience.

---

[39] Martin, Ralph, *The Fulfillment of All Desire* (Steubenville, Ohio, *Emmaus Road Publishing*, 2006) pg. 55
[40] Ps 111:10

It is then that we see who we really are - weak creatures infested with sin, buffeted by the winds of inordinate desire and the flames of uncontrolled passions. We not only see the sins of the world, but our own sins, and we are thrown into confusion, grief, even terror.

For some of us, it is the first time in our life that we realized the most sublime of all truths - we need a Savior!

These are only some of the influences that will cause the soul in the first mansions to gradually develop a whole new worldview, one that is dramatically expanded to include the spiritual realm and all of the implications of its existence. Consequently, our constricted worldview gives way to a much bigger picture of life - a picture that includes the reality of evil and the horror of sin, the consequences of our choices, the shortness of life, the reality of judgment, heaven and hell.

All of these things will begin to matter as we approach the threshold of the second mansion.

## *Vital Virtue*

*Humility*

*"Nothing else, however elevated, perfects the soul which must never seek to forget its own nothingness. Let humility be always at work, like the bee at the honeycomb, or all will be lost.*

*"But, remember, the bee leaves its hive to fly in search of flowers and the soul should sometimes cease thinking of itself to rise in meditation on the grandeur and majesty of its God.*

*"It will learn its own baseness better thus than by self-contemplation, and will be freer from the reptiles which enter the first room where self-knowledge is acquired.*

*"Although it is a great grace from God to practice self-examination, yet 'too much is as bad as too little,' as they say; believe me, by God's help, we shall advance more by contemplating the Divinity than by keeping our eyes fixed on ourselves, poor creatures of earth that we are."*

*(St. Teresa of Avila, Interior Castle, 1, 2, 9)*

## Opportunities for Advancement

In the first mansions, perseverance is everything. For this reason, Teresa recommends most emphatically that people in the first mansion commit themselves to the Mother of God and ask Her to do for them what they are unable to do for themselves - namely persevere.

She also advises that "anyone who wishes to enter the second mansion will be well advised as far as his state of life permits, to try to put aside all unnecessary affairs."[41]

---

[41] *Interior Castle*, pg. 41

## *For Reflection*

1. What "snakes and vipers and poisonous creatures" have you dragged into your mansion? Is there anything among these "many bad things" that need to be addressed in the sacrament of confession?

2. A distorted worldview is a problem that doesn't go away with the first mansion, but can persist throughout our journey. Take a moment to assess your worldview. Is it a Godly worldview, a worldly view, or a combination of both? How might your worldview be impacting your spiritual life? Is there something you can do today to begin to change the way you look at life to make it a more God-fearing point-of-view?

3. Acquiring true self-knowledge takes courage because it requires us to put aside our rationalizations and excuses and denials and see ourselves for who we really are. Conducting a daily examination of conscience at the end of the day is a good way to begin this process. Monthly confession is also a great habit to get into. What other steps might you take to come to terms with yourself?

______________________________________________

______________________________________________

______________________________________________

______________________________________________

______________________________________________

______________________________________________

CHAPTER TWO

# THE SECOND MANSION

Before we venture further into the mansions of the soul, it's important to note that a person does not stay in one mansion at a time but can move between mansions immediately ahead or behind. Also, a person does not stay in a mansion for any particular length of time. The speed of their travel is completely dependent upon how generously they are willing to surrender themselves to the will of God.

Now we are ready to learn about the second mansion of the soul, which is known as the "great battleground." Those who enter here have stepped into the arena where they will engage, perhaps for the first time in their life, in genuine spiritual combat.

At this point, the soul has become accustomed to the "sound" of the Lord's voice from prayer and can hear Him "speak" to them.

"His appeals come through the conversations of good people, or from sermons, or through the reading of good books; and there are many other ways . . . in which God calls us," Teresa teaches. "Or they come through sicknesses and trials, or by means of truths which God teaches us at times when we are engaged in prayer; however feeble such prayers may be, God values them highly."[42]

The soul struggles to respond to God because it is still greatly hampered by its weaknesses and sinfulness, which is why Teresa believes souls in this mansion have a much harder time than those in the first Mansion.

"Here the understanding is keener and the faculties are more alert, while the clash of arms and the noise of cannon are so loud that the soul cannot help hearing them. For here the devils once more show the soul these vipers - that is, the things of the world - and they pretend that earthly pleasures are almost eternal; they remind the soul of the esteem in which it is held in the world, of its friends and relatives, of the way in which its health will be endangered by penances (which the soul always wants to do when it enters this Mansion) and of impediments of a thousand other kinds."[43]

The "clash of arms" and "noise of cannon" are their unchecked passion which the devil uses to tempt and torment the soul; thus, the soul is truly at war with both itself and the world.

---

[42]Avila, Teresa, *Interior Castle*, translated and edited by E. Allison Peers (New York, NY, *Doubleday Books*, 1989), pg. 47

[43] Ibid, pg. 48

As Father Dubay explains: "They are still engaged in worldly past times, half giving them up and half clinging to them. They see imperfectly, and they act imperfectly, but nonetheless some growth has occurred. God is calling them ceaselessly and they are able to hear Him now. In the first mansions, they were both deaf and dumb, notes Teresa, but now the message is beginning to get through. Yet these people are not able to do the divine bidding immediately, for they are weak and irresolute."[44]

There is a tug-of-war going on within them, he continues. "The world's tug is experienced in several ways; earthly pleasures remain attractive, and they appear as though almost eternal. The soul finds it hard to give up esteem in the world and a selfish clinging to family and friends. In the opposite direction, God's tug is likewise felt in diverse manners . . . ."

It is the battle between nature and grace, which is why it's so important to understand that the two are polar opposites.

"Nature indeed is wily and betrays many through its deceits and crafty ways, and has always self as its end," writes Thomas Kempis. "On the other hand, grace walks with simplicity, turning aside from all that appears evil. Grace is not concerned with its own profit, but with what may benefit others."[45]

---

[44] Dubay, Thomas, S.M., *Fire Within* (San Francisco, CA, *Ignatius Press*, 1989) pg. 83

[45] Kempis, Thomas, *Imitation of Christ* (New York, NY, *Catholic Book Publishing Co.*, 1969) pg 216-217

Nature loves to be honored and respected, but grace refers all honor and reverence to God.

Nature loves leisure, but grace is never idle and gladly embraces toil.

Nature would rather rebel than obey while grace is always happy to live under God's command and those to whom He gives authority.

Nature loves rarities, luxuries, and expensive things but grace finds joy in the humble and the simple.

Nature loves to horde and clings to its possessions. Grace is completely unselfish and believes it is more blessed to give than to receive.

Nature expects to be paid for its labors and does nothing for free; grace seeks no reward except from God alone.

When misfortune arises, nature is quick to complain. Grace bears poverty with peace and constancy.

Nature loves to boast about its many friends; grace loves even its enemies.

Between these two opposing forces a mortal combat rages, which is why the soul in this mansion spends most of its time falling into sin and climbing back out.

The good news is that these conflicts are already producing hidden benefits to the soul who will persevere.

"If then, you sometimes fall, do not lose heart, or cease striving to make progress, for even out of your fall God will bring good . . . "[46]

Every fall that the soul manages to overcome deepens humility and teaches us to be more reliant upon God. As painful as these falls might be, they are slowly building the two great pillars of the spiritual life - trust in God and distrust in self.

However, the soul in this mansion is still an infant in the practice of the Gospel virtues such as humility, obedience, love and patience. For this reason, their prayer life is still in the first stage. Prayer advances in tandem with the depth of our commitment to the Gospel. As we embrace the Christian life of perfection more deeply, our prayer will begin to move into the second stage.

The important thing is not to waste time looking for lofty favors from God in prayer, such as locutions and apparitions because the soul is still an infant in the spiritual life.

"You may think that you will be full of determination to resist outward trials if God will only grant you inward favors," Teresa warns. "His Majesty knows best what is suitable for us; it is not for us to advise Him what to give

---

[46] *Interior Castle*, pg. 51

us, for He can rightly reply that we know not what we ask."[47]

For now, our job is to exercise ourselves in the virtues, to persevere in daily prayer, and to remind ourselves that no one enters the Kingdom "but those who do the Father's will."[48]

However, God is a good and wise Father. He woos the soul in this mansion with just enough supernatural delight to offset the anxiety caused by the person's interior conflicts.

"The Lord is so anxious that we should desire Him and strive after His companionship that He calls us ceaselessly, time after time, to approach Him . . ."[49]

He will speak to us very boldly at times, mostly through the conversation of good people, from homilies, or the reading of spiritual books."

Prayer, although still in the first stage, can be sweet to the point of tears in this mansion because God is already at work healing the damaging effects of our prior sin-life. Abortion, broken marriages, resentments, and grudges are all wounds to the spirit much like cuts and abrasions wound the body. These injuries must be lanced, drained, and healed.

---

[47] Ibid

[48] Matt. 7:21

[49] *Interior Castle*, pg. 47

Once done, the soul can experience an almost unearthly bliss and lightness of spirit. The person feels better than ever before, from the inside out, rejuvenated and alive once again in places where they once knew only shame or despair. They fall head over heels in love with God. Not only is He real, He has become their hero, their helper, their healer - their Savior.

Consequently, the soul is able to see Him everywhere - in everything and everyone. It's a whole new reality - like waking up on another planet.

In spite of the conflicts, the internal wars, the constant relapses, the most frequent song of the soul in this mansion is: "God is alive! Alleluia!"

But there are pitfalls everywhere. In addition to the everyday battle with the three evils - the self, the devil, and the world - the devil is very active here. He will try to lure the soul back into the world by pretending that earthly pleasures are almost eternal, Teresa warns.

"They remind the soul of the esteem in which it is held in the world, of its friends and relatives, of the way in which its health will be endangered by penances (which the soul always wants to do when it enters this mansion) and of impediments of a thousand other kinds."[50]

## *Fuel for the Journey*

*Understanding the Three Evils*

---

[50] *Interior Castle*, pg. 48

When it comes to evil, knowledge is power. Satan wants nothing more than to convince us that he doesn't exist and until we learn otherwise, we will remain spiritually vulnerable. If we have any hope of moving forward in this journey, the soul in the second mansion must acquire a more mature attitude toward evil, understand how it operates in our lives, and learn how to conquer it.

For starters, we need to understand that the devil is not the only evil we will confront on this journey. In fact, he's not even the most powerful evil. St. John of the Cross did us the huge favor of listing the three evils in ascending order, from the weakest to the most powerful, so we can have some idea of what we're up against.

"The world is the enemy least difficult to conquer; the devil is the hardest to understand; but the flesh is the most tenacious, and its attacks continue as long as the old self lasts."[51]

Let's take a look at these three evils, beginning with the most powerful.

***The Flesh***

Of all the people in our lives in which we take pleasure, one person always holds first place - ourselves.

---

[51] John of the Cross, *The Collected Works of St. John of the Cross*, translated by Kieran Kavanaugh, OCD and Otilio Rodriquez, OCD (Washington, DC, *ICS Publications*, 1991) pg. 720

"There is no one, no matter how limited in talent or good qualities, who does not love his own excellence, and who does not try, in one way or another, to make it shine forth to himself and to others."[52]

We have a true talent for spontaneous exaggeration about our good qualities, but rarely a word to say about the bad. Our need for notice often makes us want a higher place in the world than we're due. We cannot tolerate being overlooked, criticized or ridiculed, and God forbid someone should slander our good name!

In other words, we're full of pride, self-love, and willfulness, which is the exact opposite of the Redeemer we're supposed to be imitating. Jesus was obedient to the death for love of us; we obey the boss because we want to get paid. Jesus offered no defense when wrongly accused; our accusers barely finish speaking and we're already giving them a piece of our mind. Jesus rarely displayed anger, even toward the men who were crucifying Him; we lose our temper for things as minor as being cut off in traffic.

Is it any wonder this evil is the hardest to vanquish? Who wants to look in the mirror and see all their pride, their many faults and weaknesses for which they have no one to blame but themselves?

As we journey toward union with God, which will take place in the seventh mansion, we will be engaged in constant mortal combat with the enemy of the flesh, against which we have been given the surest and most

---

[52] Father Gabriel of St. Mary Magdalen, OCD, *Divine Intimacy* (Rockford, Ill., *Tan Books and Publishers, Inc.*, 1996) pg. 315

powerful weapon in our spiritual arsenal - grace. With God, all things are possible, and it will be with His grace alone that we will learn how to conquer ourselves.

### *The Devil*

St. John gives the devil second place only because his power is limited by God who will never permit him to tempt us beyond our strength. The big problem with this enemy is his cunning, which is beyond human comprehension. Satan capitalizes on our weaknesses and attacks us where we are the least able to defend ourselves. Unless we're making a serious attempt to develop Christian virtues in ourselves, particularly humility and purity, we're leaving ourselves wide open to attack.

### *The World*

Being in third place doesn't make the evil of the world any less formidable an enemy. It has its own peculiar power, which is all about our attachments to things, people, status - whatever can be used to weaken our attachment to Christ.

As Father Gabriel writes, "There is also attachment to one's comfort, to certain sensible satisfactions, to one's own opinion or reputation. There is a real mushroom-bed of appetites and disordered inclinations from which the soul will not free itself . . . because it is attached to the meager selfish satisfaction which it finds in these wretched things."[53]

We are supposed to love God above everything else, and with our whole heart, mind, and strength. "If the heart is occupied with inordinate attachments to self or creatures, it is clear that it cannot love God with all its strength, which is divided between God and self, between God and creatures."[54]

This doesn't mean we can't enjoy legitimate pleasures because that would be impossible. Man was created to be happy. But we're supposed to love these things in the measure assigned by God, and with a view toward pleasing Him, not for our own selfish satisfaction.

St. John teaches that "To gain complete mastery over any of these three enemies, one must vanquish all three; and in the weakening of one, the other two are weakened also."[55]

When faced with evil, there is no need to cower. We must run to God just like the child who runs straight to its parent to do what it cannot do for itself. We must be careful never to try to conquer these evils with our own resources or think we can acquire enough knowledge or strength to go it alone. This is why we must always be at work developing within ourselves an ever deeper humility that comes from true self-knowledge. This will enable us to see ourselves for who we really are - weak

---

53 *Divine Intimacy*, pg. 233
54 *Divine Intimacy*, pg. 236
55 *Collected Works*, pg. 720

and incapable creatures who can do no good except that which the Lord achieves in us through His grace.

## ***Roadblock***

*The Need for Human Respect*

One of the greatest weaknesses of a soul in the second mansion is its inability to let go of its worldly stature and the esteem of its friends. Little does it know how vulnerable it becomes to the devil because of this weak spot.

To illustrate just how dangerous this vice can be, let us examine one of the most famous dreams of St. John Bosco entitled, "The Road to Hell."[56]

In the dream, St. John was walking along a wide and beautifully paved road that was lined with roses and hedges. As he moved along, he saw that many of his students were following him.

"As I was looking at them, I noticed now one, now another fall to the ground and instantly be dragged by an unseen force toward a frightful drop, distantly visible, which sloped into a furnace," St. John described.

---

[56] *Forty Dreams of St. John Bosco* (Rockford, Ill., *Tan Books and Publishers, Inc.,* 1999)

He asked his guide what was making them fall and the guide said, "Take a closer look."

Saint John looked and realized that there were traps everywhere, very close to the ground and well concealed. "Unaware of the danger, many boys got caught, and they tripped and they would sprawl to the ground," he wrote. "The ground traps, fine as spider webs and hardly visible, seemed very flimsy and harmless, yet to my surprise, every boy they snared fell to the ground."

He was astonished that such a filmy fiber could trip up so many of his best boys. Investigating further, he was even more horrified to see that the thin thread was being worked by the devil himself, who remained hidden while trapping the boys.

"But what is it?" he asked the guide.

"A mere nothing," the guide said. "Just plain human respect."

Just plain human respect.

It's something we hardly think about, or even notice, and yet this was what made Pontius Pilate prefer to crucify the Son of God than face an angry mob. This was the sin of Herod who beheaded John the Baptist because he was more afraid of going back on his word in front of his dinner guests.

Just plain human respect.

It's that uneasy feeling inside that makes us keep quiet when we know we should speak up. It's what makes us feel more comfortable rationalizing blasphemy as "art" or "free speech" than denouncing it for what it is - blasphemy. It's that telltale little whisper at the back of the mind that asks, "What will people think?"

The need for human respect can be the single most powerful vice afflicting people in the early mansions of the soul. Referred to by many spiritual masters as the most universal of all human failings, the need for human respect is what makes us forsake all that we know to be right and embrace evil simply because we don't want to be laughed at or called "fanatic!" We lose our focus and want to be respected by people more than by God.

The most prevalent form of this vice in modern society goes by the familiar name of "political correctness." It's a social dictatorship that brandishes anyone who doesn't agree with a certain way of thinking. It's what tells us it's wrong to think like a Christian in a pluralistic society where immorality goes by the name of "tolerance" and grave sin masquerades as a "choice".

It takes guts to buck this tide, to oppose abortion, contraception, same-sex marriage, assisted suicide, especially in a culture where these evils are being promoted as "a woman's choice", "equal rights" and "death with dignity". The so-called "low information voters" remain duped until someone like us speaks up and says, "But wait! This is wrong!" even if we're later dismissed as backward fanatics.

Speak up we must because the price of silence is too high! We risk being tripped up like so many of St. John's students, pulled into the very gates of hell by this seemingly minor vice.

"Those who are potential leaders in the Catholic pro-life movement are not slaves of human respect," wrote the late Father John Hardon. "I use the word 'slaves' deliberately. Most people are slaves of human respect . . . . Those who live out what they believe are willing to be opposed in living out their faith . . . . To heroically live out what we believe is not child's play."[57]

Blessed Titus Brandsma, OCD, who went to his death in Dachau, knew this truth only too well. “He who wants to win the world for Christ must have the courage to come into conflict with it,” he once said.[58]

It's easier said than done, however. In our culture, the pressure to conform is enormous; and the poorly catechized are even more vulnerable in their ignorance about the faith and the moral teachings of the Church.

---

[57] Hardon, John, "A Catholic's Responsibility as Leader in the Right to Life Movement," accessed on 01/18/14 at http://www.therealpresence.org/archives/Pro_Life/Pro_Life_001.htm.

[58] Steichen, Donna, "Human Respect in a Barbaric Age", *Touchstone Magazine*, August 13, 2013, accessed 01/18/14 at http://www.touchstonemag.com/archives/article.php?id=13-08-013-v#ixzz2qlpzcDRR

"Having no guide, they are swept along by the currents of opinion prevailing in the surrounding culture," writes Catholic author Donna Steichen.

"But not only the ignorant sin out of human respect," she warns. "Even catechized and committed Catholics can find their faith eroded by the culture. People who set out to 'engage the world' may end by marrying it, sometimes without realizing that they have crossed that fateful line."[59]

Crossing that line can mean the difference between authentic Catholic teaching or "cafeteria style Catholicism". It can mean the difference between acceptance or rejection, employment or unemployment, wealth or poverty. But if crossing that line means betraying our Christian beliefs, it's better to suffer here than in eternity.

Jesus has guaranteed this! "Blessed are you when they insult you and persecute you and utter every kind of slander against you because of me. Be glad and rejoice, for your reward is great in heaven."[60]

Those who are in the early mansions must pray for the strength to live what they believe - even if that means being opposed.

"I would never have the gall to say what I am about to say unless I had tasted a sliver of what I am sharing with you," Fr. Hardon writes. "Those who are willing to live heroic Catholic lives are literally happy to suffer in the following of Christ. Why? Because like Christ, they

---

[59] Ibid

[60] Matt. 5:11-12

know that suffering is the language of charity. Those who love Jesus Christ are to live like Christ."

The good news is that those of us who live the sacramental life have a guaranteed source of the kind of superhuman strength we need to overcome the interior cowardice that makes us want to cave in the face of ridicule. We have the sacraments! When we fall victim to the need for human respect, we can find healing and new hope in the sacrament of Reconciliation. To keep up our strength and sustain us in the battle, we can feed upon the Body and Blood of Our Lord every day of the week if we so desire.

We have everything we need to follow Christ as we ought - and to change the world as we do.

## Vital Virtue

Perseverance

*"What most distresses souls of good will who are seriously trying to live a spiritual life, is to find themselves falling so many times, despite their continual and sincere resolution. . . .*

*"The real evil is not so much in falling as in failing to rise. . . . The annoyance felt by so many souls when they see themselves continually falling is not the fruit of humility, but of pride. . . . They rely too much on themselves . . . . In the plan of Providence these falls are for the definite purpose of convincing us that we are miserable creatures. . . .*

*"To have the courage to persevere in the struggle, especially when we fall repeatedly - either as a result*

*of our imperfection and frailty, or because God permits it in order to humble us more -0 we must join to humility an immense confidence in the divine help. . . .*

*"The more convinced we are that God is calling us to sanctity, and that our personal resources are insufficient for attaining it, so much the more should we be convinced that God will furnish us with the help needed to answer His call."*

*(Fr. Gabriel of St. Mary Magdalen, OCD, Divine Intimacy, pg. 883-885)*

## *Opportunities for Advancement*

St. Teresa gives us good advice about how to proceed to the third mansion.

First, we must be faithful to daily prayer and in overcoming our human will in order to let God's will reign more and more in our lives.

"All that the beginner in prayer has to do - and you must not forget this, for it is very important - is to labor and be resolute and prepare himself with all possible diligence to bring his will into conformity with the will of God.[61]

About the devil, we must be resolute, she says. "If the devil sees that he [the soul] has firmly resolved to lose his life and his peace and everything that he can offer

[61] *Interior Castle*, pg. 51

him rather than to return to the first mansion, he will very soon cease troubling him."[62]

Stand firm, find good Christian friends, and don't hesitate to lean on them.

"It is a very great thing for a person to associate with others who are walking in the right way; to mix, not only with those whom he sees in the rooms where he himself is, but with those whom he knows have entered the rooms near the center."[63]

## *For Reflection*

1. In what areas of your life are you experiencing the battle between nature and grace? In your need for more possessions, honors, friends? Identify these areas, then ask God to grant you whatever grace you need to conquer these vices.

___

___

___

___

___

___

___

[62] Ibid, pg. 50
[63] Ibid, pg. 49

2. How does the sin of human respect impact *your* world? Where are you the most challenged in this area - at work, at home, in school? List some of the feelings you experience when confronted with disdain or mockery from someone who doesn't share your beliefs, then ask Jesus to heal you and strengthen you for the battles ahead.

_______________________________________________

_______________________________________________

_______________________________________________

_______________________________________________

_______________________________________________

_______________________________________________

_______________________________________________

3. How do you confront the constant cultural pressure to be politically correct? Do you try to avoid it, cave in to it, or say "bring it on!"? What are you most afraid of when it comes to speaking up about what is right? To be laughed at, proven wrong, argued with? Pray to the Holy Spirit and ask to be strengthened in the virtue of courage.

_______________________________________________

_______________________________________________

_______________________________________________

_______________________________________________

_______________________________________________

_______________________________________________

_______________________________________________

4. How resolute are you about things that matter to you? On a scale of one to 10, with 10 being the highest, grade yourself on how firmly you persevere - are you

weak (1-2), somewhat wobbly, (3-4) sometimes strong (5-8) or always strong (9-10). Think about the last time you "caved" to pressure of some kind and felt compelled to do what you didn't want to do. What made you falter?

How might you call upon God next time to lend you whatever strength you need to endure?

_______________________________________________

_______________________________________________

_______________________________________________

_______________________________________________

_______________________________________________

_______________________________________________

_______________________________________________

CHAPTER THREE

# THE THIRD MANSION

Souls who have reached the third mansion are described by St. Teresa as being "most desirous not to offend His majesty; they avoid committing even venial sins; they love doing penance; they spend hours in recollection; they use their time well; they practice works of charity toward their neighbor; and they are very careful in their speech and dress and in the government of their household if they have one."[64]

This description sounds much more perfect than it really is, however. As Teresa warns, our piety is not quite as deep as it should be. We're still very attached to our own opinions, possessions, reputation. Although we have truly pious desires, "words are not enough, any more than they were for the young man when the Lord told him what to do if he wishes to be perfect . . . we all say we desire it, but if the Lord is to take complete possession of the soul, more than that is necessary."[65]

---

[64] Avila, Teresa, *Interior Castle*, translated and edited by E. Allison Peers (New York, NY, *Doubleday Books*, 1989), pg. 59
[65] Ibid

In other words, our love for God "must not be wrought in our imagination, but must be proved by works," she says.

This doesn't mean we must give up our jobs and start all kinds of spiritual apostolates. It means engaging ourselves in the serious practice of Christian virtue. And we must learn to accept the daily crosses inherent in our state in life; to obey our superiors, whether or not we agree with them; to profess our faith in the world no matter how much ridicule it might bring upon us. For persons in the third mansion, the time has come to practice what they preach.

But we're not quite there yet, which is why this mansion can be one of glaring inconsistencies. For instance, we may experience intense fervor in prayer and think we're ready to endure anything for the Lord, even to the point of death! And yet an hour later, someone may ask us to help them out at an inconvenient time and we just can't bring ourselves to oblige. If we can't put ourselves out for a friend, we certainly aren't ready to die for Christ!

Another typical failing is not wholly embracing the teachings of the Church. Perhaps we disagree with one of the Church's moral positions and instead of practicing the Christian virtue of obedience - which we must do even when we disagree with a teaching - we dissent and cause scandal within the body of the Church. If we can't obey those who the Lord has put in charge of us, what makes us think we can obey Him?

These and other contradictions are the daily fare of the soul in the third mansion. It's a kind of spiritual adolescence that in Teresa's case, lasted about 10 years, from the time of her father's death in 1542 until her conversion in 1554.

"It was a time filled with uncertainty and back and forth movement. Yet with the death of her father she returned to a truth she saw in childhood, that everything is passing. She recovered her ideals, but not without a great struggle between her prayer life and all that warred against it, between, in her words, friendship with God and friendship with the world."[66]

In this stage, we're still making excuses for ourselves and often mistakenly believe we're being persecuted for our faith rather than merely suffering due to our own imperfections.

Nowhere is this fault more obvious than in the area of our want to convert others which can be almost overwhelming at times.

"A desire for our neighbor's perfection is undoubtedly excellent," writes the great spiritual director, Father Jacques P. DeCaussade. "The interior grief we feel at the sight of his failings can be equally excellent if it originates from a pure desire to see him perfect. Yet all this can be mixed with much secret self-complacency, reliance upon our own wisdom, and severity toward our

---

[66] St. Teresa of Avila, Kieran Kavanaugh, Carol Lisi, Otilio Rodriguez, *The Interior Castle Study Edition*, (Washington, DC: *ICS Publications*, 2010) pg (interpretive notes, 3rd mansion, 1st chapter)

neighbor. Such zeal, make no mistake about it, cannot come from God, but is one of the devil's illusions thoroughly harmful to both yourself and others."[67]

We know our zeal is undisciplined if we tend to be impatient with the faults of others rather than endure them as calmly and for as long as God does. We tend to be bitter and harsh in our speech, which only turns off the person we are addressing. In spite of the beauty of the Gospel we're preaching, our unruly passions tend to make our presentation clumsy and ineffective. These same passions are like a "blackened glass . . . which prevents you from seeing things and describing them to others in their true colors."[68]

Fr. DeCaussade advises souls in this state to "Be always on your guard against this distressing tendency; cherish thoughts and sentiments that counteract such peevishness . . . make it your delight to assure others of the infinite goodness of God and the trust we should have in Him; let your behavior give them an example of virtue that is neither stiff nor embarrassing to others; take special care never to make harsh announcements . . . . When you can find nothing gentle to say, keep quiet, leaving the burden of such pronouncements to others who will find it easier than you to be rightly strict, avoiding too great leniency and too great severity alike."[69]

---

[67] DeCaussade, Jacques P., *Self Abandonment to Divine Providence* (Rockford, Ill.: *Tan Books and Publishers, Inc*., 1987) pg. 221
[68] Ibid, pg. 222
[69] Ibid, pg. 223

Undisciplined zeal has a tendency to make God (and us) more enemies than friends, an outcome which is easily mistaken for persecution. In reality, it's a backlash against our own inept handling of the situation.

At this point in our journey, we are best advised to mind our own business until we have acquired the kind of humility and prudence that makes us into effective ambassadors for Christ.

Being the neophytes that we are, we also need to stop being shocked at the faults of others because "we might well learn very important lessons from the persons who shock us"[70].

Remember, humility is everything on this journey. We will use many other fuels to propel us toward the seventh mansion, but humility will always be our "high octane". For this reason, God will subject us to other tests meant to reveal to us who we really are - and why we need Him so much.

For instance, we might experience a financial loss that causes us much more distress than we thought it would, leaving us almost inconsolable; or maybe we received a windfall and suddenly realize it's not enough for us. We can worry about our health to the point that we make our condition even worse.

"Or, God may want to use them because they are good people, to give examples of virtues to others and so

---

[70] *Interior Castle*, pg. 69

allows them to undergo some persecution in which their reputation is damaged. They become terribly unhappy and disquieted over the loss of their prestige."[71]

" . . . Often it is God's will that His elect should be conscious of their misery and so He withdraws His help from them a little - and no more than that is needed to recognize our limitations very quickly. They realize that this is a way of testing them, for they gain a clear perception of their shortcomings," Teresa writes.[72]

For this reason, she suggests that we "test ourselves before we are tested by the Lord - and it would be a very great advantage if we were prepared and had learned to know ourselves first."[73]

Tackling our interior shortcomings can feel quite formidable in the beginning, but not all is struggle in this mansion. The Lord is generous in rewarding our every effort.

"He always gives us much more than we deserve by granting us a spiritual sweetness much greater than we can obtain from the pleasures and distractions of this life."[74]

We are still too close to the first mansions and prone to fall back, so God will counter our trials with powerful

---

[71] *The Interior Castle Study Edition*, (interpretive notes, 3rd mansion, 2nd chapter)
[72] *Interior Castle*, pg. 63
[73] Ibid
[74] Ibid, pg. 67

doses of spiritual delight, as well as a few "sneak previews" of what's to come in the next mansions.

Although still in the first stage of prayer, the soul in the third mansion is approaching the threshold between natural and supernatural prayer which will occur in the fourth mansion. As a prelude to this coming change, the soul may begin to feel subtle inclinations toward more quiet, reflective prayer. They just don't feel like reciting all those prayers every day and sometimes fight with themselves to let go and just "be" with God in a kind of simple, loving awareness.

These feelings are often mistaken for temptations from the devil to stop praying, or they believe the world will end or their loved ones won't be saved if they don't say certain prayers every day. During moments such as these, if we invoke the Holy Spirit and put ourselves in His hands and the feeling remains, it's safe to leave the fate of our loved ones in His loving hands for a few minutes while we enjoy the peace of His presence. We can always return to our prayers later.

But those who are not well-versed in the ways of prayer frequently make the mistake of forcing themselves to pray like before, which stifles these impulses to higher forms of prayer.

Another crucial turning point in our spiritual life will also occur during this phase of our journey. We suddenly become aware of the incredible reality of our baptism, that God is not the "man upstairs" but is a living Person who resides by grace within our very soul. He's closer to us than our very breath, and all we need to do to communicate with Him is to turn our sights within.

This is called the practice of the presence of God and is actually a manner of praying that results in a new loving awareness of God that is no longer confined to just our prayer time. Rather, it begins to manifest throughout the day. We find ourselves silently talking to God in the car, our office, at the kitchen sink. He becomes much more "real" to us. We feel connected to Him in a new and special way as we begin to live our lives conscious of His presence at our sides.

This new intimacy with God greatly offsets them misery of our daily encounters with the weakness in our own flesh. An authentic love begins to grow between us and God.

We have a sense that great things are happening within us and that a new door is about to open in our spiritual life, but we're still hampered by our humanness. We want to soar, but our human nature is sluggish and relentlessly earthbound. As Teresa describes, human nature begins to feel like "a great load of earth."

No one wants us to fly higher than the Lord, and at some point in these first mansions, He will begin to unshackle us from the impurities that are keeping us tied to earth.

## ***Fuel for the Journey***

*The Dark Night of the Sense*

There are two phases of purification that we will undergo during the course of our journey, the first of which happens in the earlier mansions. Known as "dark nights", the phrase was first coined by St. John of the Cross who describes two distinct dark night experiences, one to purify the senses and the second to purify the spirit.

The first night, known as the dark night of the senses, aims at detaching us from disorderly attachments to sense-oriented pleasures in order to make them subject to the spirit. The second night, called the dark night of the spirit, delves deeper and is concerned with purifying the intellect and the will.

Everyone experiences these dark nights a little differently, depending on the degree of perfection God intends for each of us.

There is both an active and a passive stage of these purifications. In the first night, the active stage involves learning how to let go of our innate self-centeredness and inordinate desire for pleasures of the senses. This doesn't mean giving up everything that feels good. It means giving up the pursuit of these pleasures for their own sake rather than for God's sake.

We know we're too attached to something if we 1) use something or activity for a purpose God did not intend it to be used, such as using our speech to lie or deceive; 2) if we use something in excess, such as over-eating or drinking, and; 3) make a means into an end, such as engaging in idle chatter just for the sake of talking, which makes this chatter into a kind of idol.

It's not hard to see how easily these attachments can lead us into any and all of the seven deadly sins of pride, avarice, envy, sloth, lust, anger, and gluttony. Normally, at the time of our conversion, most of us embark on a sincere effort to overcome these sins, but we often neglect the underlying attachments that might be causing them.

Speaking of this oversight, St. John of the Cross notes how we tend to adopt many penitential practices thinking these are sufficient to purge ourselves of sin. "But these practices are insufficient if a person does not diligently strive to deny his appetites," St. John writes. "If these people would attempt to devote only half of that energy to the renunciation of their desires, they would profit more in a month than in years with all these others exercises."[75]

St. John of the Cross is by no means opposed to the senses and the pleasures they naturally afford; his beef is with the way we enjoy them.

In his book, *Fire Within*, Fr. Thomas Dubay S.M. explains: "We are so immersed in our disordered selves

---

[75] Kavanaugh, Kieran, OCD, Rodriguez, Otilio, OCD, *The Collected Words of St. John of the Cross* (Washington DC: *ICS Publications*, 1991) *The Ascent of Mount Carmel*, Book 1, Chapter 9, No. 4 pg. 136

that we assume that sense pleasures are their own end, that we were created for them, that we may pursue them aside from the very reason they exist: to plunge us into unending Beauty, Joy, Love and Truth. Hence, our sense life is properly oriented when it sparks prayer." [76]

When we hear exquisite music, taste delectable food, gaze upon a panoramic vista, our first response should be to adore the Creator of these things. In other words, we should be more enthralled with the God who created the thing than the thing itself.

But arriving at this level of purity of spirit doesn't happen overnight. It takes time, daily conversion of heart, perseverance in prayer and in reception of the sacraments, and, most importantly, a willingness to accept the trials that occur in the natural course of our lives which is usually how our dark nights are experienced.

The passive stage of the night of the senses is God's work and usually involves detaching us from the desire to pursue the spiritual life because it pleases us and makes us feel good. This is a very common and critical step for those who decide to take their spiritual life more seriously because it is our senses that lead us into error and false forms of worship. The dark night of the senses weans us off of the "feel good religion" we experienced at the beginning of our spiritual walk and urges us into a more mature spirituality.

---

[76] Dubay, Thomas, S.M., *Fire Within* (San Francisco, CA, *Ignatius Press*, 1989) pg. 146

As St. John of the Cross explains, at first, the "soul finds its joy in spending lengthy periods at prayer, perhaps even entire nights; its penances are pleasures; its fasts, happiness; and the sacraments and spiritual conversation are its consolations. Although spiritual persons do practice these exercises with great profit and persistence, and are very careful about them, spiritually speaking, they conduct themselves in a very weak and imperfect manner."[77]

Because it feels so good and brings so much satisfaction, the soul tends to be practicing its faith more for itself than for God. This is why, while they are proceeding happily along this joyful road, God may suddenly "turn out the lights." The sweet dew of devotion dries up. We feel dead inside, empty. Once we could meditate for hours, now we can hardly string together two good thoughts.

"He leaves them in such dryness that they not only fail to receive satisfaction and pleasure from their spiritual exercises and works, as they formerly did, but also find these exercises distasteful and bitter," St. John writes.[78]

St. Teresa of Avila endured an 18 year-long dry spell and St. Therese of Lisieux rarely had any consolation in prayer from the moment of her entrance into Carmel until her death.

---

[77] *The Collected Works of St. John of the Cross, The Dark Night*, Book 1, Chapter 2, No. 3, pg. 362

[78] Ibid, Book 1, Chapter 9, No. 3, pg. 376

Dryness in prayer can be the result of many things, such as illness or spiritual mediocrity, which is why St. John gives us three signs of an authentic sensory night, all of which must be present: 1) the soul suddenly derives no consolation from the things of God; 2) the person agonizes over this deprivation, believing it is somehow their fault; 3) the person is powerless to pray as they did before, no matter how hard they try.

These dry spells may come and go, or be continuous, and although they may feel harsh, they are tremendously important because they teach us to stop reducing our faith to what we can feel and understand. God wants to give us much more, and is now urging the soul to move into more advanced stages of prayer such as contemplation.

In this new form of prayer, God begins to communicate directly to the soul, bypassing the senses, which is why contemplation usually "feels" dry at first. This experience can be initially disturbing, even frightening, but it is always illuminating and transforming because when prayer is dry and distasteful, we learn how to pray for God's sake, rather than our own.

And in the process, we empty ourselves a little more and take another step closer to the real God, who is beyond our imagination or perception. What might seem like a tomb for our senses is actually the dawning of a new day for the spirit.

# *Roadblock*

*Attachment to Sin*

We are growing by leaps and bounds even though it might not seem like this at first. In the spiritual life, we often see things more clearly when we look back on them.

But we have not yet become a proficient in the realm of the spirit and one of the most common reasons is that we are still clinging to some aspect of our former sin life. We no longer commit mortal sins, but there are some venial sins we just can't seem to conquer and may even *like* to commit.

This is especially true regarding sins of the tongue such as repeating gossip, snapping at loved ones, making rude or nasty remarks.

"It is not enough . . . to guard one's tongue from these and similar kinds of nastiness [public insult and abuse, venomous slander in secret]," St. Bernard of Clairvaux warns. "Even slight offenses must be avoided, if anything may be termed slight that is directed against a brother for the purpose of hurting him, since merely to be angry with one's brother makes one liable to the judgment of God."[79]

---

[79] Bernard of Clairvaux, *On the Song of Songs*, Volume 2, page 106, as quoted by Ralph Martin in *The Fulfillment of All Desire*, pg. 113.

He also cautions us to be careful how we respond when offended.

" . . . Do not immediately rush, as a worldly person may do, to retaliate dishonorably against your brother; nor, under the guise of administering correction, should you dare to pierce with sharp and searing words one for whom Christ was please to be crucified."[80]

He gives a long list of unacceptable responses such as making resentful noises, muttering or murmuring complaints, adopting a "sneering air" or indulging in "the loud laugh or contempt" and knitting the brow in "menacing anger."

Yes, it's hard to do, but with God all things are possible and all we need to do is call upon Him and He will send us the grace to prevail.

The problem is that deep down inside, many souls in this stage of the journey don't really *want* God's help. They want to enjoy the feeling of victory they get from putting another "in their place" by delivering a retort just as nasty.

St. Francis de Sales teaches us that nourishing affection for venial sins "weakens the powers of our spirit, stands in the way of God's consolations, and opens the door to temptations."[81]

While we must be careful not to become overly scrupulous by thinking everything we do is sinful, we

---

[80] Martin, Ralph, *The Fulfillment of All Desire*, pg. 104
[81] Ibid pg. 114

must be willing to root out whatever is causing us to hold on to that particular sinful habit which we confess over and over again in the confessional.

This is why spiritual masters such as the great Dominican theological Father Reginald Garrigou-Lagrange suggest that we take steps to identify and root out our predominant fault.

"The predominant fault is a defect in us that tends to prevail over the others, and thereby over our manner of feeling, judging, sympathizing, willing, and acting. It is a defect that has in each of us an intimate relation to our individual temperament."[82]

For instance, some of us may be prone to gluttony, sloth, anger or pride, and these lead us to sinful behaviors that "feel right" because they are suited to our natures.

This fault must be rooted out because the devil is very aware of it and uses it to stir up trouble within us and hold us back from progressing in the spiritual life.

How do we discern this fault?

First, it is very important to understand that one is never a good judge of their own character.

"Self-love deceives us," says Father Lagrange, who advises us to seek the help of a spiritual director or good

---

[82] Lagrange-Garrigou, Reginald, O.P., *The Three Ages of the Interior Life* (Rockford, Ill., *Tan Books and Publishers*, Inc.) Volume one, page 314

friend when embarking on the quest to identify our predominant fault.

Of course, we should not even think of doing this without first asking for the guidance of the Holy Spirit.

"Lord, make me know the obstacles I more or less consciously place in the way of the working of Thy grace in me. Then give me the strength to rid myself of them, and if I am negligent in doing so, do Thou deign to free me from them, though I should suffer greatly."[83]

Then we should gently begin the task of asking ourselves a few pointed questions such as:
"Toward what do my most ordinary preoccupations tend, in the morning when I awake, or when I am alone? Where do my thoughts and desires go spontaneously?"[84]

"What is generally the cause or source of my sadness and joy?"[85]

The predominant fault may also be recognized by the temptations the devil most frequently assails us with for he especially likes to attack us in the area of this weakness.

Beware that the predominant fault often takes on the appearance of a virtue. For instance, when we fall do we beat ourselves up and believe we're doing this because

---

[83] *The Three Ages of the Interior Life*, pg. 316
[84] Ibid
[85] Ibid, pg. 317

we want to be better, or is it because of an underlying pride that can't bear to see its own weakness?

Once we have isolated our predominant fault we must get to work conquering it, which is done by three principal means: prayer, examination of conscience, and a sanction.

As Father Lagrange recommends, our prayer must be sincere. He quotes the prayer of Blessed Nicholas of Flue who used to pray: "Lord, take from me everything that hinders me from going to Thee. Give me all that will lead me to Thee. Take me from myself and give me to Thyself."

Next, we must conduct a daily examination of conscience and, as St. Ignatius of Loyola suggests, write down the number of times each week that we have yielded to our predominant fault.

Next, we must impose a sanction or penance upon ourselves each time we fall to this defect. This penance can take the form of a prayer, a moment of silence, an exterior or an interior mortification of some kind.

We must remember that in this stage of our journey to God, our virtues are more like natural good inclinations than true and solid virtues because "we still seek ourselves too much and do not live sufficiently for God" which prevents the fountain of grace from flowing fully into our souls.

Father Lagrange also warns us to be on our guard against pusillanimity, a deliberate lack of boldness, which may try to convince us to give up because this fault is too powerful to be overcome.

Not so! With grace, we can overcome it, just as St. Augustine taught us in accordance with the findings of the Council of Trent. "God never commands the impossible; but in giving us His precepts, He commands us to do what we can, and to ask for the grace to accomplish what we cannot do."[86]

In order to overcome our affection for sin, to weed out our predominant fault and remain docile to the Lord's methods of purification, we must never give up the fight.

"It has been said that the spiritual combat is in this case more necessary than victory, for, if we dispense ourselves from this struggle, we abandon the interior life, we no longer tend toward perfection. We must not make peace with our faults."[87]

## *Vital Virtue*

*Obedience*

*Obedience is called the "queen" of all virtues because it relies on the quality dearest to the heart of God - humility. Nothing can test one's humility more than*

---

[86] *The Three Ages of the Interior Life*, pg. 319
[87] Ibid

*having to obey someone appointed by God to be our superior - whether or not we agree with them.*

*This is why obedience has always been the test of the saints used by the Church to determine the depths of a person's holiness.*

*We should accept every opportunity to practice obedience with the only exception being if we are asked to commit a sin. The regular practice of obedience strengthens our ability to renounce our own will and bend to the will of God.*

*If we obey only because we agree with someone or something, this is mere human obedience which is a good act in itself, but not supernatural. To obey only because God wills whatever our superior commands is supernatural obedience.*

*This isn't always easy, which is why Pope Pius XII once said, "Obedience is the burden of the strong."*

*With the help of His grace, instead of repeating Lucifer's "I will not serve!" we can echo the words of the Master who bowed His head in the Garden of Olives and said, "Not my will, but thine."*

## *Opportunities for Advancement*

Teresa gives good advice to those who wish to journey beyond the third mansion - mainly to keep our eyes in our own plate.

"Let us look at our own shortcomings and leave other people's alone."[88]

We must be careful not to "expect everyone else to travel by our own road, and we should not attempt to point them to the spiritual path when perhaps we do not know what it is."[89]

People in this mansion should also groom within themselves the "queen" of all virtues - obedience - in order to avoid an "isolated and self-sufficient style of existence". The last thing we want to do is follow our own will, "for it is in this way that we usually do ourselves harm."[90]

In conclusion, "Those who live in this third dwelling place have to recognize that they need not only to offer themselves generously to the Lord but to recover from their failings. They have to become engaged in a more difficult task: accepting that God has plans that go far beyond one's present project, generous though it may be, and letting Him take the initiative, especially when it is a surprise and upsets one's own strategies."[91]

## *For Reflection*

1. Can you spot any "glaring inconsistencies" in your spiritual life? These are times when you are most likely

---

[88] *The Interior Castle*, pg. 69

[89] Ibid

[90] Ibid, pg.68

[91] *The Interior Castle Study Edition*, (interpretive notes, 3 mansion, 2 chapter)

to act imperfectly, and without a Christ-like response. Jot them down, then ask the Holy Spirit to help you to identify the "triggers" that are making you fall.

_______________________________________________

_______________________________________________

_______________________________________________

_______________________________________________

_______________________________________________

_______________________________________________

_______________________________________________

2. What sins do you repeat over and over again in the Sacrament of Reconciliation? Is it the need to gossip, to eat, drink, spend too much, gamble? This is a good way to discern any attachments to sin that might be plaguing your spiritual life. Confess this sin and ask the priest to recommend what steps you can take to overcome this fault.

_______________________________________________

_______________________________________________

_______________________________________________

_______________________________________________

_______________________________________________

_______________________________________________

3. Have you ever identified your predominant fault? Ask the Holy Spirit to help you do so. This process may take a while, and remember to seek out the advice of your spiritual director, confessor, or even just a good and faith-filled friend or family member who knows you well enough to help you find this fault. Once identified, ask the Holy Spirit to help you develop a plan to confront and overcome this fault.

______________________________________________

______________________________________________

______________________________________________

______________________________________________

______________________________________________

# CHAPTER FOUR

# THE FOURTH MANSION

You are about to enter one of the most pivotal of all the mansions, the one "which the greatest number of souls enter," St. Teresa tells us.[92]

It is here that we cross the threshold between natural and supernatural prayer. What began so subtly in the third mansion becomes more pronounced here as we begin to experience a new kind of communication with God, one that is not felt in the senses or understood by the mind. Yet it happens - here and there - like random flashes of heat lightening on a warm summer night.

"As these mansions are now getting closer to the place where the King dwells, they are of great beauty and there are such exquisite things to be seen . . . that the understanding is incapable of describing them in any way accurately without being completely obscure to those devoid of experience," Teresa writes.[93]

---

[92] Avila, Teresa, *Interior Castle*, translated and edited by E. Allison Peers (New York, NY, *Doubleday Books*, 1989), pg. 59

[93] Ibid, pg. 72

There is no set time when a person will reach this stage in their journey; nor is there any specific length of time a person must reside in the first three mansions before they arrive here. At this point, it's all up to the generosity of the soul.

"It seems that, in order to reach these mansions, one must have lived a long time in the others; as a rule one must have been in those which we have just described, but there is no infallible rule about it, as you must often have heard, for the Lord gives when He wills and as He wills and to whom He wills, and, as the gifts are His own, this is doing no injustice to anyone," she explains.[94]

Souls who reach this stage will have some common characteristics. They will be devoted to God and the Church, attend daily Mass when able and regularly avail themselves of the Sacrament of Reconciliation. Devotion to the Eucharist, to the Mother of God, to the Saints, will be an everyday part of their life. They sincerely struggle to avoid all sin, to grow in virtue, and to be a worthy servant of God. Despite being in a sometimes painful process of purification, which may or may not involve trials such as reversals of fortune or failing health, they are determined to keep the faith. Not even long periods of dry prayer can turn them aside from the God they have come to know and to love with a profound and genuine affection.

---

[94] *Interior Castle*, pg. 73

Ever so slowly, and without the soul even being aware, it has begun to make the turn away from coming to God for its own pleasure to doing so for His.

Generally speaking, this is the state the soul is in when it may begin to receive the first touches of infused contemplation.

"Infused contemplation is a divinely given, general, non-conceptual loving awareness of God," explains Father Thomas Dubay.

"There are no images, no concepts, no ideas, no visions. Sometimes this awareness of God takes the form of a loving attention, sometimes of a dry desire, sometimes of a strong thirsting. . . . It can be delicate and brief, or in advanced stages burning, powerful, absorbing, prolonged. Always it is transformative of the person, usually imperceptibly and gradually but on occasion obviously and suddenly."[95]

As fantastic as it may sound, it begins in a very unspectacular way and may at first be mistaken for a kind of daydreaming. We feel as though we "zoned out" for a few minutes but can remember no concrete thoughts or images. We just "weren't there."

These are the first experiences of the action of God who begins to do more of the work in prayer. He progressively takes over the will and then the intellect and imagination, something St. Teresa referred to as the "suspension of the faculties." God bypasses the senses and begins to communicate directly to the soul. The

---

[95] Dubay, Thomas, S.M., *Fire Within* (San Francisco, CA, *Ignatius Press*, 1989) pg. 86

faculties "are relieved of the ordinary human necessity of working at thoughts, ideas and affections."[96]

Unless one is schooled in the ways of advancing prayer, they are apt to overlook these signs and will attempt to return to their vocal prayers and thus suppress what the Holy Spirit is trying to do. This is why Teresa cautions that "knowledge and learning are a great help in everything."[97]

Teresa describes two different kinds of infused prayer that will occur at this stage: the Prayer of Recollection and the Prayer of Quiet.

### *Prayer of Recollection*

We will almost always experience the Prayer of Recollection first, and then the Prayer of Quiet. This recollection is not that which we could accomplish by focusing on a meditation or thoughts that arouse devotion within us. This is an infused and gentle awareness of God that is not produced by human effort. We suddenly feel drawn to be alone with God because it is He who is drawing us away from the things of the world.

"It is a form of recollection which also seems to me supernatural," Teresa explains, "for it does not involve remaining in the dark, or closing the eyes, nor is it dependent upon anything exterior. A person involuntarily closes his eyes and desires solitude . . . the

---

[96] *Fire Within*, 86-87
[97] *The Interior Castle*, pg. 75

senses and all external things seem gradually to lose their hold on him, while the soul, on the other hand, regains its lost control."[98]

These experiences are delicate in the beginning, which is why beginners are advised to be well instructed because they are apt to miss what is happening and will stifle these movements by returning to active prayer.

### *Prayer of Quiet*

St. Teresa describes this prayer as a quiet, deep, and peaceful happiness of the will but without any human understanding of what it is.

"The state resembles an interior and exterior swoon; for the exterior part . . . doesn't want any activity. . . . They feel the greatest delight in their body and a great satisfaction in their soul. They feel so happy merely with being close to the fount that they are satisfied even without drink. It doesn't seem there is anything else for them to desire."[99]

The kind of delight experienced in this prayer is so different from earthly pleasures that it is hardly possible to express it in images or ideas. When we experience this infusion, whole blocks of time seem to just disappear. We are aware of nothing around us, or within us. One minute we were kneeling in prayer, and the next thing we know 20 minutes have vanished from the

---

[98] *The Interior Castle*, pg. 85

[99] Teresa of Avila, *The Way of Perfection Study Edition* (Washington, DC, *ICS Publications*, 2000) pg. 338

clock. Although we have no recollection of what happened to us during that time, we are completely certain that we were with God. In fact, the peace we experienced will often last for days afterward.

"The quiet is felt in differing degrees at different times," Fr. Dubay explains. "It may last a long time, even for a day or two. It follows then, that one can enjoy this interior awareness even though engaged in exterior activities that require the attention of the mind."[100]

These infusions start off subtly and grow in intensity as the soul becomes more accustomed to it.

Naturally, the soul can begin to long for these experiences, which is why a good number of problems can and do arise in this stage.

## *Roadblock*

*Lack of Receptivity*

By the time a soul has reached this stage in their journey to God, they are becoming strong and stalwart, exactly the kind of soul Satan wants to be rid of before it does him too much harm.

"I earnestly warn such people not to enter up on occasions of sin, because the devil sets much more store by one soul in this state than by a great number of souls to whom the Lord does not grant these favors. For those in this state attract others, and so they can do the devil

---

[100] *Fire Within*, pg. 88

great harm and may well bring great advantage to the Church of God," Teresa warns.

"He may see nothing else in them except that His Majesty is showing them especial love, but this is quite sufficient to make him do his utmost to bring about their perdition. The conflict, then, is sterner for such souls than for others and if they are lost their fate is less remediable."[101]

Because souls at this stage are more advanced and knowledgeable about the ways of Satan, however, the evil one tends to set up more subtle traps to ensnare them and bring them down - especially those who are paying too little attention to cultivating the virtue of humility.

For instance, it's only natural for a soul to be "wowed" by these experiences and long for them to happen again. Thus, it is easy to forget that infused contemplation is always a gift from God and not something we can control.

"It is not we who decide when this change shall take place," writes Father Dubay. "It is God Who gives the new communion, and thus it is He who takes the initiative. Hence it would be foolish for a person to decide 'I like this idea of infused prayer; I'll begin it tomorrow'."[102]

This isn't hard to imagine, especially in our secular culture.

---

[101] *Interior Castle*, pg 92
[102] *Fire Within,* pg. 87

"In our consumerist-productionist societies there is a tendency to take for granted that we are in control of making happen whatever we want to have happen and of determining how it will come about. This expectation results in resistance to the kind of receptivity required for prayer."[103]

A lack of receptivity can quickly turn into a gaping pothole on the road to God, something that can even happen inadvertently if we're not careful.

For instance, there are a plethora of Buddhist and Eastern methods of meditation that call for the blanking of the mind in order to induce altered states of consciousness. Mistaken by many as prayer, someone who is too anxious for more advanced spiritual experiences may turn to these practices, thinking they can somehow "speed up" the process.

These methods involve the use of a mantra that is constantly repeated in order to "drown out" all thoughts, impulses and feelings so that the mind becomes a total blank. Some require a person to practice this technique 20 minutes in the morning, and 20 minutes at night. The goal is not to dialogue with God, as is the goal of Christian prayer, but to maintain this mental void throughout.

As the *Catechism* teaches, "In the battle of prayer, we must face in ourselves and around us erroneous notions of prayer. Some people view prayer as a simple

---

[103] *Fire Within*, pg. 90

psychological activity, others as an effort of concentration to reach a mental void."[104]

St. Teresa warns that efforts to stifle thoughts often result only in awakening thought all the more. These efforts also prove that we are focusing more on ourselves and our own wants rather than on the Lord's.

"How can a person be forgetful of himself when he is taking such great care about his actions that he dare not even stir, or allow his understanding and desires to stir, even for the purpose of desiring the greater glory of God or of rejoicing in the glory which is His? When His Majesty wishes the working of the understanding to cease, He employs it in another manner and illumines the soul's knowledge to so much higher a degree than any we can ourselves attain that He leads it into a state of absorption, in which, without knowing how, it is much better instructed than it could ever be as a result of its own efforts, which would only spoil everything. God gave us our faculties to work with, and everything will have its due reward; there is no reason, then, for trying to cast a spell over them - they must be allowed to perform their office until God gives them a better one."[105]

Some popular mind-blanking movements, such as Centering Prayer, have taken it so far as to suggest that St. Teresa actually endorsed this kind of prayer. In truth, she did just the opposite.

---

[104] *Catechism of the Catholic Church* (Boston, MA, *St. Paul Books & Media*), No. 2726
[105] *Interior Castle*, pg. 89

"Taking it upon oneself to stop and suspend thought is what I mean should not be done; nor should we cease to work with the intellect, because otherwise we would be left like cold simpletons and be doing neither one thing nor the other. When the Lord suspends the intellect and causes it to stop, He Himself gives it that which holds its attention and makes it marvel [note: He doesn't blank the mind, but takes control of its thought processes and infuses those He wishes the soul to contemplate]; and without reflection it understands more in the space of a Creed than we can understand with all our earthly diligence in many years. Trying to keep the soul's faculties busy and thinking you can make them be quiet is foolish."[106]

Some people take this so far as to be falling into the grips of a heretical doctrine known as Quietism which taught that there was to be no human activity at all in prayer - no consolation, no yearnings for happiness, no prayer of petition.

As a result, "quietism promoted a gross inertness in a spiritual void," Fr. Dubay writes. [107]

This is not at all what St. Teresa taught. Instead, she suggested that when God is leading a soul into this prayer, a person might attempt to stop all discursive reasoning, yet not try to suspend the understanding or cease all thought.

---

[106] Teresa of Avila, *The Book of Her Life* (Washington, DC, *ICS Publications*, 1976) pg. 121
[107] *Fire Within*, pg. 89

There is room for human activity in the prayer that occurs in the fourth mansions, but it is gentle and simple activity.

"The most we should do is occasionally, and quite simply, to utter a single word, like a person giving a little puff to a candle, when he sees it has almost gone out, so as to make it burn again . . ."[108]

Reducing prayer to a technique means to divorce it from life, something that St. Teresa never advocated. In the first three mansions she insists on daily fidelity as a condition for prayer growth in any stage of development. In mansions four through seven she emphasizes how this growth in prayer brings about an ever deepening commitment to the Gospel. The two go hand in hand.

And when they do, the transformation is impressive.

The soul becomes "less constrained in matters relating to the service of God than it was before and give it much more freedom. It is not oppressed, for example, by the fear of hell, for, though it desires more than ever not to offend God (of Whom, however, it has lost all servile fear), it has firm confidence that it is destined to have fruition of Him. A person who used to be afraid of doing penance lest he should ruin his health now believes that in God he can do everything, and has more desire to do such things than he had previously. The fear of trials . . . is now largely assuaged because he has a

---

[108] *The Way of Perfection*, pg. 340

more lively faith, and realizes that if he endures trials for God's sake, His Majesty will give him grace to bear them patiently, and sometimes even to desire them, because he also cherishes a great desire to do something for God."

The soul's view of itself and the world around him are also vastly changed. "The better he gets to know the greatness of God, the better he comes to realize the misery of his own condition; having now tasted the consolations of God, he sees that earthly things are mere refuse so, little by little, he withdraws from them and in this way becomes more and more his own master. In short, he finds himself strengthened in all the virtues and will infallibly continue to increase in them unless he turns back and commits offenses against God."[109]

## *Fuel for the Journey*

*Detachment*

Because this growth is dependent upon God and our response to His grace, one of the best ways to facilitate this growth is to continue to work on detaching ourselves from all that binds us to earth.

"The goal of the process of detachment is not to stop loving the things and people of this world, but, quite the contrary, to love them even more truly in God, under the reign of Christ, in the power of the Holy Spirit. Things and people become even more beautiful and delightful when we see them in this light," writes Ralph Martin.

---

[109] *Interior Castle*, pg. 91

However, he goes on to warn: "There are almost always painful dimensions to this process of "letting go" in order to love more, but it's the pain of true healing and liberation. Christian detachment is an important part of the process by which we enter into a realm of great freedom and joy."[110]

As Martin points out, God the Father explained why we need to go through the process of detachment to St. Catherine of Siena.

"For created things are less than the human person. They were made for you, not you for them, and so they can never satisfy you. Only I can satisfy you . . ."

The Father goes on to explain that a soul suffers when it loses something it has lost. "These souls have in one way or another identified with the earth in their love, and so they have in fact become earth themselves."

Some identify with wealth, others with their children, or status.

"The more disordered their love in possessing, the greater is their grief in loss," He says.

"Had they held these things as lent to them rather than as their own, they could let them go without pain. They suffer because they do not have what they long for. For,

---

[110] Martin, Ralph, *The Fulfillment of All Desire* (Steubenville, Oh., *Emmaus Road Publishing*, 2006) pg. 205

as I told you, the world cannot satisfy them, and not being satisfied, they suffer."[111]

What freedom we would have if we adopted this advice from our Heavenly Father to see all of the things we own as having been lent to us by Him rather than being our own! After all, didn't our job and all the skills we used to acquire our possessions also come from Him?

When we learn to do this, we develop within ourselves an interior freedom of heart that puts its trust not in things - in possessing or keeping what we have, or longing for what we don't have - but in the Father's care.[112]

We cannot soar to the heights God has in store for us while still being chained to the earth and all its trappings. How can we get anywhere if one unexpected tax bill finds us collapsing into a fit of worry and despair?

This is why a person stifled by a myriad of earthly attachments is unable to advance very far in the spiritual life.

"God brings one thus far as a pledge of great things He has in store, but if He sees the person 'return to earth', He refrains from showing him the secrets of His kingdom."[113]

---

[111] Ibid, pg. 206-207
[112] Ibid, pg. 208-209
[113] *Fire Within*, pg 93

Not that we could see those secrets very clearly anyway because attachments, like all sin and imperfection, have a clouding effect on the soul. St. John of the Cross compares the presence of attachments to the smattering of dirt on a clean window. Instead of seeing the full radiance of the sun, we're allowing only a small glow to get through because our windows are smeared with too many worldly concerns - job, family, possessions, inter-personal relationships. Letting go of these concerns doesn't mean forsaking family and friends or being careless on the job - it means learning how to care for them for God's sake and not our own.

If we don't follow this advice, these things can become "little gods" to which we are constantly made to answer. They are forever ordering us around, demanding satisfaction, which inadvertently saps our mental, physical and spiritual energy.

How do we know if we're suffering from an inordinate attachment?

St. John of the Cross gives us three signs:

***The first sign*** is if the activity or thing is diverted from the purpose God intends for it. For example, if one uses the tongue to lie in order to get ahead on the job, this shows an inordinate attachment to one's own gain, not to the glory of God.

***The second sign*** is an excess of use. As soon as we go too far in eating, drinking, recreating, speaking or working, we show that there is something disordered in our activity.

This can mean buying more clothes that we need, working more than necessary, traveling more extensively than we ought. These are some of the more obvious signs of inordinate attachment, but there are many less recognizable forms, such as being too attached to our own opinion or reputation, to little vanities and comforts, to unrestrained curiosity and idle chatter.

***The third sign*** is making the means into an end. For instance, when we engage in idle talk just for the sake of talking, or eat just for the sake of eating, etc

Selfish clinging to things or creatures focuses too much attention on ourselves rather than on God, thus drawing us away from Him. It prevents us from preferring what pleases God to what pleases ourselves. Most of the distractions we suffer in prayer are due to these disordered concerns and desires. Our hearts remain divided between love of God and love of mammon. Prayer too often feels more like a tug-of-war than a quiet visit to our eternal Fatherland.

A further concern is that disordered attachments almost always give rise to venial sins, or at least to deliberate imperfections when we willingly yield to them, even though it may be only in matters of the slightest importance. Being too concerned about our reputation can lead us into sins of vanity, envy, or avarice. Idle chatter is too often the doorway to gossip or at least the wasting of time. Being too impressed with our own opinions can make us uncharitable and argumentative. Requiring too much comfort and luxury can make us lazy and morally weak.

However it's important to remember that this detachment comes in stages and not all at once. God knows we are not able to disentangle ourselves without a lot of effort.

As Teresa advises: "I don't say that all those who experience this prayer must by necessity be completely detached from the world. At least, I would like them to know what is lacking and that they humble themselves and try to go on detaching themselves from everything; if they don't, they will remain in this state."[114]

Too many do, she sadly laments, stating that this is the reason the numbers of spiritual people are not much more numerous.

## *Vital Virtue*

*Courage*

*The more a soul loves God, the more courageous it will be in undertaking any work, no matter how laborious, for love of Him.*

*. . . The virtue of fortitude does not exempt us from the fear and alarm which invade our nature when faced*

---

[114] *Way*, pg. 343

*with sacrifice, danger or . . . the imminent danger of death. But fortitude is exercised by the will; hence, it is possible to perform courageous acts in spite of our fear. In these cases, courage has a twofold function: it conquers fear and faces the difficult task. . . .*

*It is not within our power to suppress the sensible fear which we inherit with our fallen nature . . .but we can prevent it from taking possession of our will and paralyzing our acts. We must act energetically, forcing ourselves in the name of God to do what we should, and not stopping to argue with fear."*

*Many souls say, 'I have not the strength to accomplish such an act.' But let them begin and put forth some effort!*

*. . . Courageous acts performed when we have no courage are more pure and more supernatural; they are purer because they afford no place for feelings of pride; they are more supernatural because they are based, not on the resources of nature, but on those of grace.*

*(Divine Intimacy, Father Gabriel of St. Mary Magdalen, pg. 862-863)*

## ***Opportunities for Advancement***

St. Teresa tells us that at this stage in a person's spiritual life they have grown so much in virtue that they can only continue to grow in them unless they resort to deliberate mediocrity and neglect.

But that doesn't mean we can afford to be complacent! St. Teresa stresses three conditions for growth into the fifth mansion:

1) Never give up the habitual practice of prayer.
2) Further detach oneself from everything.
3) Seek greater solitude, without neglecting one's duties, and give the Lord an opportunity to work.

## *For Reflection*

1. How many of the common characteristics listed on page 84 of souls who have reached this mansion can you identify in yourself? Have you ever experienced infused prayer? If so, what was your reaction? If not, how do you feel about the possibility of this happening to you in prayer? Is it something you look forward to, or does it make you feel anxious? Do you regard these experiences of God as something you have to earn or as a free gift from God?

_______________________________________________

_______________________________________________

_______________________________________________

_______________________________________________

_______________________________________________

_______________________________________________

_______________________________________________

2. Take a moment to reflect on your level of receptivity to all that God might want to give you. Are you completely open to His will in your life? Are you

willing to give up control, even of your spiritual/prayer life? If not, what is holding you back?

______________________________________________
______________________________________________
______________________________________________
______________________________________________
______________________________________________
______________________________________________

3. Being human, we all have a tendency toward inordinate attachments. What are you *too* attached to? Your loved ones, possessions, comforts, future plans, bank account? Identify these attachments, then consider how they might be preventing you from giving God more leeway in your life.

# Chapter Five

# THE FIFTH MANSION

Just as prayer develops slowly and through progressive stages of spiritual development, so each mansion is a gradual development of the one before. Whereas the faithfulness of the soul in the fourth mansion was rewarded with the beginnings of infused prayer, the soul who is entering the fifth mansion has begun to give even more of itself to the Lord, which is why He will, in turn, give more of Himself to the soul.

"But observe, daughters, that if you are to gain this, He would have you keep back nothing," Teresa writes. "Whether it be little or much, He will have it all for Himself, and according to what you know yourself to have given, the favors He will grant you will be small or great."[115]

The generous soul who has reached the fifth mansion is a person so intensely taken with the Lord that

[115]Avila, Teresa, *Interior Castle*, translated and edited by E. Allison Peers (New York, NY, *Doubleday Books*, 1989), pg. 97

she is now completely forgetful of herself. God is now everything to her.

"We find here evidence of the reciprocal interinfluence of deepening prayer and detachment from self-centeredness," writes Father Thomas Dubay. "Just as the latter frees one for progressively greater love, precisely as one is less and less cluttered by finite things, so as one grows in love, one effortlessly grows in the inner liberty of other-centeredness."[116]

For this reason, at some point during the transition from the fourth to the fifth mansion, the profound silence of the prayer of quiet begins to give way to a much deeper absorption in God called the prayer of union or spiritual betrothal.

Unlike what will happen in the seventh mansion when the soul fully understands the great favors God is granting it, this is not the case with the prayer of union. Instead, Teresa says the soul becomes much like St. Paul at the moment of his conversion - blind and dumb. It is akin to being asleep in all of our human faculties, but not to God.

"He makes them lose consciousness of everything but Him. They don't understand, however, the way in which they are aware of God, nor can they describe it. This loss of consciousness of the world never lasts long - twenty minutes to a half hour or less - but it does seem

---

[116] Dubay, Thomas, S.M., *Fire Within* (San Francisco, CA: *Ignatius Press*, 1989) pg. 95

that much less time passes to the one experiencing the union."[117]

In spite of being in this dream-like state, the soul experiences a consolation, a sweetness, a delight that is incomparably greater than what was experienced in the Prayer of Quiet.

"This prayer is a glorious foolishness, a heavenly madness . . . Often I had been as though bewildered and inebriated in this love . . . the soul would desire to cry out praises and is beside itself . . .it cannot bear so much joy . . ."[118]

The length of this absorption is brief, never longer than a half hour. But what this prayer lacks in duration it makes up for not only in intensity, but also in a profound certainty of the divine presence. In fact, this very certainty is a sign that the experience is from God.

The experience is also indelible as the person who receives this favor will never forget it and will always remember the exact day and hour that it was received. Such profound experiences of God are life-changing. As Father Dubay notes, the person in this mansion continues to be transformed and emerges from these absorptions "with a consuming desire to praise God and to die a thousand deaths for His sake."

---

[117] St. Teresa of Avila, Kieran Kavanaugh, Carol Lisi, Otilio Rodriguez, *The Interior Castle Study Edition*, (Washington, DC: *ICS Publications*, 2010) Interpretive Notes, 5th mansion, 1st chapter, No. 4

[118] *Way,* Chapter 16

The soul has become like a stranger to the earth as it tastes a Divine elixir that compares to nothing that can be found on earth. But this doesn't mean the soul loses its peace. Deep inside, it experiences a profound calm.

Yet at the same time, this person feels acutely that he cannot serve God well enough, and he is pained that there are so few men and women in the world who care about the Lord and so many who offend Him.

However, this grief is infused and not simply the result of our meditations, Fr. Dubay explains. "It reaches so deeply into one's being that it "seems to tear it to pieces and grind it to powder."

This is all part of that death to self that is so necessary in order for us to rise in the glory of the Lord into whom we are being transformed.

St. Teresa of Avila explains the meaning behind this spiritual process in her famous analogy about the little silkworm.

"The silkworm is like the soul which takes life when, through the heat which comes from the Holy Spirit, it begins to utilize the . . . help God gives to us all and to make use of the remedies which He left in His Church - such as frequent confession, good books and sermons . . ."

When the little worm is fully grown, "it starts to spin its silk and to build the house in which it is to die.

This house may be understood to mean Christ . . . Let us hasten to perform this task, and spin this cocoon. Let us renounce our self-love and self-will, and our attachment to earthly things. Let us practice penance, prayer, mortification, obedience, and all the other good works that you know of."[119]

If we take this advice, we will find ourselves within this fifth mansion where God takes hold of the ugly little silkworm lying dead within its silken tomb and unites it to Himself in the prayer of union. In that brief, flashing instant, the little worm is totally transformed into a brilliant white butterfly.

"Oh! Greatness of God . . .that a soul should come out like this after being hidden in the greatness of God, and closely united with Him for so short a time - never . . . for as long as half an hour!"[120]

As awe-inspiring as this new prayer sounds, receiving it is not nearly as important as the steadfast practice of virtue, particularly that of love of God and neighbor.

"When I see people very diligently trying to discover what kind of prayer they are experiencing and so completely wrapped up in their prayers that they seem afraid to stir or to indulge in a moment's thought, lest they should lose the slightest degree of the tenderness . . .which they have been feeling, I realize how little they understand of the road to the attainment

---

[119] *Interior Castle*, pg. 105
[120] Ibid, pg. 106

of union. They think that the whole thing consists in this. But no . . .what the Lord desires is works."

Teresa believes that we can only know for certain how much we love God by our practice of love of neighbor.

"Because our nature is so corrupt we cannot love our neighbor with any kind of perfection unless this love of neighbor has God as its root. But the only way we can measure our love of God is by our love of neighbor. God so loves this virtue that He will replay our efforts to practice it by increasing in a thousand ways the love we have for Him."[121]

As explained by Edith Stein, aka St. Teresa Benedicta of the Cross, the great 20th century martyr who was converted after reading St. Teresa of Avila's autobiography, our love for our fellow humans is the measure of our love for God.

"But it is different from a natural love of our neighbor. Natural love goes out to this one or that one who may be close to use through the bond of blood or through a kinship of character or common interests. The rest then are 'strangers' who 'do not concern' us, who, it may be, eventually come to be repulsive, so that one keeps them as far away as possible from contact with us. For the Christian, there are no such 'strangers'. Rather, he is the 'neighbor', this one who stands before us and who is in greatest need of our help; it doesn't matter

---

[121] *The Interior Castle Study Edition*, Interpretive Notes, 5th Mansion, 3rd Chapter, No. 4

whether he is related to us or not; whether we 'like' him or not; whether is 'morally worthy' of help or not. The love of Christ knows no bounds; it never stops, it does not shrink back from ugliness and dirt. He came for the sake of sinners and not for the sake of the just. If the love of Christ lives in us then we will, like Him, go out after the lost sheep."[122]

This primacy of love is what makes Christian mysticism different from other forms of mysticism. "It is a profoundly interpersonal relationship of love between the divine and human persons."[123]

And what a love it is! "The saints know what it is like to be in love, a love immeasurably beyond what worldlings label as love. The delight is intense because the love is intense."[124]

One can almost feel the intensity of the love Teresa had for God when she wrote: "My King, I beseech you, that all to whom I speak become made from your love . . . This soul would now want to see itself fee - eating kills it; sleeping distresses it . . . nothing other than you can give it pleasure any longer . . . and I would desire to see no other persons than those who are sick with this sickness I now have."

But in order to realize this kind of unimaginable love, we must be willing to undergo a complete death to self,

---

[122] Ibid, No. 5
[123] Ibid, Interpretive Notes, 5th Mansion, 4th Chapter, No. 1
[124] *Fire Within*, pg 95

exactly the kind that accompanies a progressive following of the Gospel of Christ.

## *Fuel for the Journey*

*Poverty of Spirit*

This death to self is known as poverty of spirit, a state we only achieve after being stripped of every pretense until we stand before God as we truly are - naked, powerless and alone.

None of us start out on this journey wanting to be who we really are - powerless beings who are wholly dependent upon God - but this is where we must eventually end up.

Poverty of spirit is not just one virtue among many. Rather, it is the foundation of all others. To love, to have faith, to hope, can only be accomplished perfectly when we have achieved at least some degree of poverty of spirit.

"Poverty of spirit is a necessary ingredient in any authentic Christian attitude toward life," writes Johannes B. Metz.[125]

In fact, it's no accident that Jesus named this as the first beatitude.

---

[125] Metz, Johannes B., *Poverty of Spirit* (Mahwah, NJ: *Paulist Press*, 1998) pg. 21

"What is the sorrow of those who mourn, the suffering of the persecuted, the self-forgetfulness of the merciful, or the humility of the peacemakers; what are these if not variations of spiritual poverty. This is the doorway through which many must pass to become an authentic human being."[126]

This is also the place our pride would rather avoid because it's just too terrifying to be that dependent on someone else. A host of "what ifs" spring up from the depths of our being that are strangely difficult to suppress.

"What if God wants something different for me than what I had in mind?" or "What if He does this or that to my life?"

The questions are never-ending, but they can all be summarized in one statement.

"I don't think I know God well enough to trust Him that much."

This is why Metz calls poverty of spirit the true meeting place between God and man. It is only when we "let go and let God" that we really get to know Him. The depths of His faithfulness, His love, His mercy, can only be sounded with the rod of experience.

Which is why Satan goes out of his way to prevent us from reaching this place in our spiritual formation. "This

---

[126] *Poverty of Spirit*, pg. 21

ancestral refusal to face our lot is a standing temptation for man," Metz writes.

From the beginning of our history, Satan has been whispering in our ears, "Go ahead! You'll be like God!" He encourages us to think too highly of ourselves and our own strength, especially in regard to spiritual matters. "Look how well you've done! Look how far you've come!" he applauds us and we bask in our own progress, quickly forgetting the words of Christ, "You can do nothing without me."[127]

And so, whether we like it or not, to become man means to become poor, to have nothing to brag about before God.

Of all creation, humans are the only ones who are not sufficient unto themselves. For example, other animals live in "mute innocence and cramped necessity . . .with no future horizons. They are what they are from the start. The law of their life and being is spelled out for them and they resign themselves to these limits without question."

Man, however, is the only creature who is "plagued by unending doubts and restless, unsatisfied hearts. Of all creatures, we are the poorest and the most incomplete. Our needs are always beyond our capacities and we only find ourselves when we lose ourselves."[128]

---

[127] John 15:5
[128] *Poverty of Spirit*, pg. 25

But in the final analysis, "man has one of two choices: to obediently accept his innate poverty or to become the slave of anxiety."[129]
St. Terese of Lisieux is one of the best modern examples of how to live in true poverty of spirit. Calling it the "little way of spiritual childhood", she knew it was not her grandiose feelings of devotion that attracted God to her soul.

"The thing that pleases Him most is that I love my littleness and poverty and have a blind hope in His mercy."

St. Therese shows us how to live the Christian definition of self-love, which is the acceptance and love of one's own limitations, but which must include a confidence in God as the Guardian of our weakness.

"God does not undermine our humanity," Metz writes. "He protects and insures it. His truth makes us free."[130]

Only with God can we be who we really are - creatures totally dependent upon His mercy. We need not fear our smallness but should instead treasure it, because this is the only place where God and man can truly meet.

Of all men, Jesus was the greatest example of poverty of spirit.

---

[129] *Poverty of Spirit*, pg. 27
[130] Ibid, pg. 20

"Did not Jesus live in continual dependence on Someone else?" Metz akss. "Was not His very existence hidden in the mysterious will of the Father? Was he not so thoroughly poor that he had to go begging for his own personality?"[131]

Jesus was no great artist, statesman, genius.

"He was a frighteningly simple man," Metz writes.

Misery was not His choice, it was his lot, "which is the only way we really taste misery, for misery has its own inscrutable laws. With nothing of his own to provide security, the wretched man has only hope - the virtue so quickly misunderstood by the secure and the rich. They confuse it with shallow optimism and childish trust in life, whereas hope emerges in the shattering experience of living 'despite all hope' (Roman 4:18). Sinful man really hopes when he no longer has anything of his own. Any possessions, material wealth, or personal strength tempt him to vain self-reliance."[132]

No one experienced the poverty of being human more deeply and more excruciatingly, than Jesus Christ, which is especially apparent during His Passion.

"Everything was taken from Him . . . even the love that drove Him to the cross. No longer did he savor his own love, or feel any spark of enthusiasm. His heart gave out and a feeling of utter helplessness came over

---

[131] *Poverty of Spirit*, pg. 25
[132] Ibid, pg. 38

him. Truly, he emptied himself . . . . The Son of Man reached his destiny, stretched taut between a despising earth that rejected him and a faceless heaven thundering God's 'no!' to sinful mankind. Jesus paid the price of futility. He became utterly poor."[133]

In doing so, Jesus really endured our lot. "He stepped down from his divinity," Metz writes. "He came to us where we really are - with all of our broken dreams and lost hopes . . . "[134]

Yet this was how He taught us the "wonder of empty hands." It is only the man who has nothing but God alone, who has everything.

When we become poor in spirit, we become like a Trojan horse, seemingly empty inside, yet filled with the power of God. But this extreme might comes with a price - the surrender of our own will, our own power. It is only in the discovery of utter weakness that we will find the meaning of true strength.

At this stage in our spiritual journey, nothing can fuel us toward the transforming union with God that we seek more assuredly than this progressive impoverishment of our deepest selves.

And nothing can hold us back - or even make us fall back - faster than the lack of it.

---

[133] *Poverty of Spirit*, pg. 13
[134] Ibid, pg. 14

# *Roadblock*

*Self-Reliance*

As Teresa explains, "We must never have confidence in ourselves"[135] because to do so will inevitably lead to carelessness on our part, and that carelessness can become a formidable roadblock on our journey.

"Christian souls, whom the Lord from has brought to this point on your journey, I beseech you, for His sake, not to be negligent, but to withdraw from occasions of sin - for even in this state the soul is not strong enough to be able to run into them safely, as it is after the betrothal has been made . . . . For this communication has been no more than . . . one single short meeting and the devil will take great pains about combating it and will try to hinder the betrothal.

"Afterward, when he sees that the soul is completely surrendered to the Spouse, he dares not do this, for he is afraid of such a soul as that, and he knows by experience that if he attempts anything of the kind he will come out very much the loser and the soul will achieve a corresponding gain."[136]

In spite of how far we have come in our journey, a person in the fifth mansion can still fall back. Teresa writes about people she has known who achieved a high degree of spirituality that fell victim to the subtle snares

---

[135] *Interior Castle*, pg. 122
[136] Ibid, pg. 120

the devil lays for souls who come this close to the Lord. Satan will marshal all the powers of hell to stop a single soul from achieving betrothal because that soul has the ability to draw thousands to the Lord. Teresa uses the example of saints such as Dominic, Francis, and Ignatius to illustrate just how many souls can be saved by a single saint - in the saint's lifetime and for hundreds of years after their death.

The closer we get to God, the more formidable an adversary we become to Satan.

But how can a soul who has come this close to God, who is obviously desiring nothing but the will of God, be deceived? And how does the devil go about ruining a soul that has gained so much?

"To the first question, my reply would be that, if this soul invariably followed the will of God, it is clear that it would not be lost,"[137] Teresa responds.

"But the devil comes with his artful wiles and, under color of doing good, sets about undermining it in trivial ways and involving it in practices which . . . are not wrong . . . " but are not perfectly aligned with God's will. A perfect example is how the devil managed to fool the Cure of Ars, as told by Fr. Ludovic-Marie Barielle.

"What would you have done if you had wanted to ensnare the Cure? Probably, you would have sent him a woman of ill repute. Yet, the Cure of Ars would have

---

[137] *Interior Castle*, pg. 121

converted her and would not have sinned. The devil is more subtle. He scrutinized the virtue of the Cure, his hatred of sin, his love for penance, his love for prayer, and that is what he came up with: 'Go to a Trappist monastery to mourn over your sins, to perform long and hard penances, to enjoy a contemplative life.' The Cure of Ars fell for it, and not once, but at least twice."[138]

What he suggested to the Cure was far from evil, but it was also far from what God willed for the saintly pastor. By appealing to the Cure's personal tastes, the devil was able to slowly darken his understanding and make him turn ever so subtly toward his own desires rather than to God's. Had the Cure continued on that path and not returned to his parish work, his self-love would have gradually become stronger the longer he indulged in his own wishes.

If this can happen to the Cure, it can happen to anyone.

As Teresa warns: " . . . There is no enclosure so strictly guarded that he cannot enter it, and no desert so solitary that he cannot visit it."

But why would the Lord allow this to happen?

Teresa believes it could possibly be "so that He may observe the behavior of the soul which He wishes to set up as a light to others for, if it is going to be failure,

---

[138] Varrielle, Ludovic-Marie, CP. CR. V., *Discernment of Spirits*, (Kansas City, MO, *Angelus Press*, 1992) pg. 45-46

it is better that it should do so at the outset than when it can do many souls harm."[139]

The Lord does not let a soul who has come so far be lost easily, however. As Teresa explains, "His Majesty is so anxious for it not to be lost that He gives it a thousand interior warnings of many kinds, and thus it cannot fail to perceive the danger."

The bottom line is that as we approach the sixth mansion, and our prayer begins to be punctuated by ever more intense mystical experiences, we must keep our eyes on the Lord and never make the mistake of having too much confidence in ourselves.

## *Vital Virtue*

*Love of God & Neighbor*

*"We cannot be sure if we are loving God, although we may have good reason to believe that we are, but we can know quite well if we are loving our neighbor. And be certain that, the farther advanced you find you are in this, the greater the love you will have for God." (St. Teresa of Avila, Interior Castle)*

*It's very easy to deceive ourselves into thinking we love God because we experience certain spiritual joys during our time of prayer. But "feelings" aren't love. The kind of love God requires is much deeper and stronger and always includes love of neighbor.*

---

[139] *Interior Castle*, pg. 122

*This is the same teaching that St. John gives in his first epistle: "We know that we have passed from death to life, because we love the brethren."*

*As Father Gabriel of St. Mary Magdalen points out, notice that John didn't say because we love God but because we love the brethren. It is fraternal charity, rather than pious feelings of devotion, that determine just how much we really love God.*

*"We should always remember that the virtue of charity is a certain participation not only in the infinite charity with which God loves Himself, but also in the immense love which He has for His creatures. . . . This is how charity unites us with Him who is charity by essence."*

*(Divine Intimacy, pg. 813)*

## *Opportunities for Advancement*

The soul who is traveling this road should be constantly vigilant and careful to observe the law of God with absolute obedience. Our only hope for safety is in this obedience and in never swerving from the law of God.

Now more than ever we are called up on to live the Gospel without compromise. From the soul in this mansion, " . . . The Lord asks only two things," St. Teresa writes, "love for His Majesty and love for our neighbor. It is for these two virtues that we must strive and if we attain them perfectly we are doing His will and so shall be united with Him."

## *For Reflection*

1. For persons who are striving toward Christian perfection, it's important to remember that the Lord gives to the soul in proportion to what the soul gives to Him. Are you giving as much as you could to the Lord? What are you holding back? Why?

______________________________________________

______________________________________________

______________________________________________

______________________________________________

______________________________________________

______________________________________________

2. Do you experience grief and sorrow for the Lord when you witness the grave sin that abounds in the world today? How do you make it up to Him?

______________________________________________

______________________________________________

______________________________________________

______________________________________________

______________________________________________

______________________________________________

3. To be truly poor in spirit, we must be willing to see ourselves for who we really are, weak and incapable of nothing but sin. When you consider yourself in this light, what feelings do you experience? Fear, dread,

anxiety? Or are you at peace, knowing that God loves all of you - even the darkest parts of you? What does this tell you about your level of poverty of spirit?

______________________________________________

______________________________________________

______________________________________________

______________________________________________

______________________________________________

______________________________________________

4. It's easy to become self-reliant in a culture where independence is so highly prized, but in the spiritual life, this can be deadly. Where might you be depending too much on yourself and your own devices to move closer to God? Are you striving to the point of anxiety? Do you get angry with yourself every time you fall? Do you take on strict penances, lengthy prayer rituals, and even deny yourself Communion for reasons other than being in a state of mortal sin? Where do you push yourself the most, and how might you be relying too much on yourself rather than the grace of God?

______________________________________________

______________________________________________

______________________________________________

______________________________________________

______________________________________________

______________________________________________

Chapter Six

# THE SIXTH MANSION

As one approaches the threshold of the sixth mansion, the soul moves into the third stage of prayer where a number of advanced experiences of God may already be occurring. Because the soul is now very close to the brilliance of the seventh mansion, even its most minute imperfections are painfully illuminated. Purification can be swift and intense at this stage, but the soul is so in love that it is willing to suffer anything if it will bring it closer to the Beloved.

"Souls in the sixth mansion are so obviously head over heels in love, a love of which the world has no cognizance of experience, that they live on the summit, so to speak," writes Father Dubay, who likens the soul in this mansion to be that of the man who is madly in love with the woman of his dreams. Everything that keeps him from her is burdensome and frustrating.

"The soul in the sixth mansion is this man (woman) in love. There are experiences of opposite drives to solitude with the Lord in prayer to plunging into the world to proclaim Him far and wide."[140]

As Teresa herself describes: "God gives these souls the keenest desire not to displease Him in any respect whatsoever, however trivial, or to commit so much as an imperfection if they can avoid doing so. For this reason alone, if for no other, the soul would like to flee from other people and greatly envies those who live, or have lived, in deserts. On the other hand, it would like to plunge right into the heart of the world, to see if by doing this it could help one soul to praise God more."[141]

Just as two lovers long to be alone with one another, so does the soul with God in this stage of its journey. But the kind of solitude it seeks is not an unhealthy withdrawal from society and turning in on oneself that is better known as isolation. Rather, it's more like two people in love who desire to be alone with one another.

"Anyone in love seeks to be alone with the dear one at frequent and prolonged intervals, but people in love likewise take a wider interest in the rest of humanity," explains Father Dubay. "Even a hermit seeks solitude for the sake of absorption in God but shuns self-centered isolation."[142]

---

140 Dubay, Thomas, S.M., *Fire Within* (San Francisco, CA, *Ignatius Press*, 1989) pg.
141 Avila, Teresa, *Interior Castle*, translated and edited by E. Allison Peers (New York, NY, *Doubleday Books*, 1989), pg. 164
142 *Fire Within*, pg. 122

Teresa of Avila viewed solitude as not only something needful for pious souls, but as necessary for anyone who wants to lead a serious prayer life. This is why she instructs souls in the first two mansions to do away with all of the unnecessary "busyness" of their lives.

"For those who hope to reach the principal Mansion [the transforming union found in the Seventh Mansion], this [solitude] is so important that unless they begin in this way, I do not believe they will ever be able to get there."[143]

This is not an easy task in today's society where silence is at a premium. No matter where we are, there's noise - traffic, voices, iPods, radios, televisions. Getting away from it can be difficult, but it's completely necessary. We simply must learn how to drastically reduce our exposure to the mass media particularly that of television, radio and film.

"If we spill out and drain our psychic energies by the endless multiplicities of images and sounds, many of them garish and deafening, we just cannot retain the inner stamina for prayer."[144]

For those who recoil at the idea of so much solitude, or doubt they'll ever manage it, St. Teresa reassures that this desire is something that grows over time. She also says that even distracted attention to the

---

[143] *Interior Castle*, pg. 41
[144] *Fire Within*, pg. 123

divine presence can transform a person from sin to virtue and eventually to heroic sanctity.

But solitude is not just about the lowering of decibels - it's also about maintaining inner peace, the kind that comes when we live a quiet and orderly life.

As St. Paul told the Thessalonians, "Live quietly and mind your own business."[145]

Why is this so important? Because people who are minding other people's business are not minding their own.

Meddling also disrupts our peace. As Fr. Dubay explains: " . . . Serious people are likely to be agitated and even shocked at all sorts of things that occur through the typical day. Their inner peace is unsettled, and prayer is hindered."

Idle talk is another nemesis of solitude. Fr. Dubay considers meddling and idle talk to be "companion traits" that are obstructions to a contemplative spirit.

"Mindful of Jesus' warning that we shall give an account on judgment day of every idle word we speak, St. Terese advised her nuns to bring to a quick conclusion any conversation that is not fruitful.

This sounds much harder than it really is when one reaches the sixth mansion because the soul in this

---

[145] 1 Thess. 4:11

stage would prefer to be "cut to pieces" than commit even a venial sin.

And for good reason. God is sweeping the soul off its feet, so to speak, with several advances experiences in prayer such as wounds of love, ecstasy, rapture, flights of spirit and levitation.

But it's important to remember that all of these experiences are considered to be infused contemplation, meaning they are a "divinely given knowing and loving of God."

"We are not concerned with merely human experiences such as those brought about by sexual union or chemical stimulation or frenzied trance. One who confuses these latter with contemplative ecstasy does not understand the latter, even if he knows something of the former."[146]

For instance, a wound of love can happen at any time, even when a person is not in prayer or even thinking about God, Teresa explains, when suddenly the soul is "awakened by His Majesty, as though by a rushing comet or a thunderclap. Although no sound is heard, the soul is very well aware that it has been called by God . . ."[147]

This "call is likened to a kind of wound that she describes as "delectable", so precious an experience that

---

[146] *Fire Within*, pg. 97
[147] Ibid, pg 135

the soul "would be glad if it were never to be healed of that wound."

The wound comes about because the soul is aware that God has called it and is indeed present, yet He does not allow the soul to enjoy Him, which causes a profound grief, "though a sweet and delectable one" she explains.

This is a far more satisfying touch of God than the powerful absorptions of the Prayers of Quiet and of Union.

"So powerful is the effect of this upon the soul that it becomes consumed with desire, yet cannot think what to ask, so clearly conscious is it of the presence of its God," she writes.

"This distress seems to penetrate to its very bowels; and that when He that has wounded it draws out the arrow, the bowels seem to come with it, so deeply does it feel this love."[148]

In order to make herself better understood, she describes God as being like a brazier from which sparks fly out and touch the soul in such a way that the soul feels its heat.

There is no way to produce this kind of phenomenon with our physical natures, nor can it be caused by our minds.

---

[148] *Fire Within*, pg. 136

Not even the devil can reproduce these feelings, she says, because nothing so delectable can be bestowed by the devil.

"He can give pleasures and delights which seem to be spiritual," she explains, "but it is beyond his power to unite pain - and such a great pain! - with tranquility and joy in the soul."

Quite the contrary. When the devil inflicts pain, it is "restless and combative".

Second, wounds of love are felt in a region of the soul over which the devil has no authority.

Third, because these wounds spawn a great determination to suffer for God's sake "and to desire to have many trials to endure, and to be very much more resolute in withdrawing from the pleasures and intercourse of this world, and other things like them," she writes.[149]

Another experience that occurs in this mansion is that of ecstasy and rapture, both of which are very similar.

A rapture comes upon a person suddenly and rapidly, rendering the person barely able to move or speak or see.

---

[149] *Fire Within*, pg. 137

"It seemed to me, the body was left so light that all its weight was gone, and sometimes this feeling reached such a point that I almost didn't know to put my feet on the ground," Teresa explains. "Now when the body is in rapture it is as though dead, frequently being unable to do anything of itself. It remains in the position it was when seized by the rapture, whether standing or sitting, or whether with the hands opened or closed."[150]

Transports or flights of spirit can also come upon a soul suddenly.

In a transport, "the soul really seems to have left the body; on the other hand, it is clear that the person is not dead, though for a few moments he cannot even himself be sure if the soul is in the body or no. he feels as if he has been in another world . . . and has been shown a fresh light there . . . . it is a fact that as quickly as a bullet leaves a gun when the trigger is pulled, there begins within the soul a flight (I know no other name to give it) which, though no sound is made, is so clearly a movement that it cannot possibly be due to fancy . . . great things are revealed to it."[151]

Teresa described levitation as one of the most disconcerting experiences she had in prayer, and it is the only experience of souls in this mansion that theologians consider to be "extraordinary".

It happened to her one day after receiving the Eucharist and greatly frightened her because she did not

---

[150] *Fire Within*, pg. 137
[151] *Interior Castle*, pg. 160

expect it and did not understand what was happening to her.

" . . . I was conscious in such a way that I could understand I was being elevated. There is revealed a majesty about the One who can do this that makes a person's hair stand on end, and there remains a strong fear of offending so awesome a God. Yet such fear is accompanied by a very great love for Him."[152]

Other experiences a soul can encounter in these later mansions concern visions, both those seen with the eyes, known as corporeal, and those seen in the mind which are called imaginative.

In a ***corporeal vision***, we see heavenly figures such as Jesus and Mary or the angels and saints with our biological eyes. Although this type of vision is the most subject to tampering by the devil, when they do come from God, they are meant to draw us to a deeper and more pure love and union with God. However, as the spiritual masters warn us, those who receive them are also in danger of being overly impressed with them and to focus on them in such a way as to block out whatever spiritual good the Lord intended.

Just as in the case of other sensory phenomena such as perceiving scents, sounds or lights, St. John of the Cross warns that corporeal visions "are a ready occasion for the breeding of error, presumption and vanity in the soul. Palpable, tangible and material as they are, they strongly affect the senses so that in one's

---

[152] Kavanaugh, Kieren, OCD, Rodriquez, Otilio, OCD, *The Book of Her Life, The Collected Works of St. Teresa of Avila*, Volume 1, , Chapter 20, page 175

judgment they seem worthwhile on account of being more sensible. A person, then, forsaking faith, will follow after these communications, believing that their light is the guide and means to the goal, which is union with God. But he more importance one gives to these communications, the further one strays from faith, the way and means."[153]

Even in this stage of the spiritual life, we are still vulnerable to falling into pride and vanity, which is why it is so easy for people who receive these visions to begin to develop a secret and special opinion of themselves, a development that the devil is only too happy to promote.

This is why St. John of the Cross recommends that we reject these visions because of these dangers.

"Even though some may be from God, this rejection is no affront to him. Nor will one, by rejecting and not wanting them, fail to receive the effect and fruit God wishes to produce through them."[154]

***Imaginative visions*** are much more reliable. These visions appear interiorly to the imagination.

As Ralph Martin explains: "The 'seeing' is not with the biological eyes, but with the 'eyes of the mind'. Interiorly, we may 'see' images of Jesus or the various

---

[153] Kavanaugh, Kieren, OCD, Rodriquez, Otilio, OCD, *The Ascent of Mount Carmel, The Collected Works of St. John of the Cross*, (Washington DC, *ICS Publications*, 1991) pg. 180-81
[154] Ibid, pg. 181

saints, or scenes of heaven or hell, angels or devils, or scenes on this earth, with strangers or people we know.

The ***interior vision*** may sometimes have a 'prophetic' character."[155]

We're given the same advice about these visions as we are about corporeal visions - ignore them.

"Yes, God works by means of imaginative visions at times, but we don't need to waste time discerning them, since, if they are from God, the effect is produced automatically in the soul. If they're from the devil or our own imagination, that is all the more reason not to pay attention to them."[156]

## ***Roadblocks***

Although it seems hard to believe that a doctor of the Church would warn us away from these visions, St. John does so with very few exceptions, mostly because he knows how prone we are to the delusions that are fueled by self-love. The time has come for this self-love to be removed from the soul where it may still be hiding to a greater or lesser degree, depending on the soul.

St. John of the Cross does an artful job of describing how the "capital" sins of pride, covetousness or avarice, lust, anger, gluttony, envy and sloth not only have a sensual component, but also a "deeply rooted existence

---

[155] Martin, Ralph, *The Fulfillment of all Desire*, (Steubenville, OH, *Emmaus Road Publishing*, 2006) Pg 319
[156] Ibid

in the depths of the human spirit, and can even hide themselves in spiritual trappings."[157]

For instance, the sin of pride can manifest itself in all kinds of spiritual practices, such as extreme fasting or other forms of penance, and even in the pursuit of perfection.

"Sometimes they minimize their faults, and at other times they become discouraged by them, since they felt they were already saints and they become impatient and angry with themselves, which is yet another fault," St. John writes.

"They are often extremely anxious that God remove their faults and imperfections, but their motive is personal peace rather than God. They fail to realize that were God to remove their faults, they might very well become more proud and presumptuous."[158]

Spiritual avarice or greed can manifest itself in the desire to have either what doesn't belong to us or to have more than what we really need.

For instance, some souls are forever attending retreats, spiritual talks, and reading books. These same souls become "peevish" or discontent if they don't get any consolation from these activities. Possessing too many spiritual things, going on too many pilgrimages and retreats, can be just as harmful as possessing too many material things because it is directly opposed to

---

[157] Ibid, pg. 338

[158] Kavanaugh, Kieren, OCD, Rodriquez, Otilio, OCD, *The Dark Night, The Collected Works of St. John of the Cross*, pg. 362-64

the kind of poverty of spirit that is necessary to enter the kingdom of God.

"Since true devotion comes from the heart and looks only to the truth and substance represented by spiritual objects, and since everything else is imperfect attachment and possessiveness, any appetite for these things must be uprooted if some degree of perfection is to be reached."[159]

Lust can also manifest itself in our spiritual life because of the close link between the spiritual and the sensory.

As St. John describes, sexual temptation can unexpectedly appear even in the higher stages of union with God.

"It happens frequently that in a person's spiritual exercises themselves, without the person being able to avoid it, impure movements will be experienced in the sensory part of the soul, and even sometimes when the spirit is deep in prayer or when receiving the sacraments of Penance or the Eucharist . . . . It may happen that while a soul is with God in deep spiritual prayer, it will conversely passively experience sensual rebellions, movements, and acts in the senses, not without its own great displeasure. This frequently happens at the time of Communion. . . ."[160]

And when it does, the devil is more than happy to make everything even worse.

---

[159] *Dark Night*, pg. 365-66
[160] Ibid, pg. 367

"To make them cowardly and afraid, he brings vividly to their minds foul and impure thoughts. And sometimes the thoughts will concern spiritually helpful things and persons . . . ."[161]

Why does he do this? To make us give up and abandon our quest for deeper union with God.

A soul must also be careful not to indulge in the sin of anger by becoming angry at ourselves - or others - for not being as perfect as believe we or they should be.

"Others in becoming aware of their own imperfections grow angry with themselves in an unhumble impatience . . . They want to become saints in a day. . . . They make numerous plans and great resolutions, but since they are not humble and have no distrust of themselves, the more resolves they make the more they break, and the greater becomes their anger. They do not have the patience to wait until God gives them what they need, when He so desires."[162]

Spiritual gluttony is another area that can plague the pious soul.

"Spiritual gluttony can express itself by desiring to do the pious practices that we prefer rather than what is most helpful and most in harmony with our state in life or in obedience to a spiritual director. Whether it be fasting, prayer, or spiritual reading, devotions or

---

[161] Ibid, pg. 368
[162] *Dark Night*, pg. 370-371

particular ministries, a desire for spiritual gratification can be an underlying motivation rather than a desire to conform ourselves to God's will."[163]

We must be careful not to allow ourselves to seek spiritual experiences rather than God Himself because once we have done so, we have begun to seek ourselves instead of God.

Souls can also experience a kind of spiritual envy when they see others who appear to be more advanced than they are.

"In regard to envy, many of them feel sad about the spiritual good of others and experience sensible grief noting that their neighbor is ahead of them on the road to perfection, and they do not want to hear others praised. Learning of the virtues of others makes them sad. They cannot bear to hear others being praised without contradicting and undoing these compliments as much as possible. Their annoyance grows because they themselves do not receive these plaudits and because they long for preference in everything. All of this is contrary to charity (1 Cor. 13:6)."[164]

Sloth is most likely to show up in beginners who shun necessary spiritual exercises to chase after those that "feel good".

"Many of these beginners want God to desire what they want, and they become sad if they have to desire

---

[163] *The Fulfillment of all Desire*, pg. 344
[164] *Dark Night*, pg. 374

God's will. They feel an aversion toward adapting their will to God's. Hence, they frequently believe that what is not their will, or brings them no satisfaction, is not God's will, and on the other hand, that if they are satisfied, God is too. They measure God by themselves and not themselves by God, which is in opposition to his teaching in the Gospel that those who lose their life for his sake will gain it and those who desire to gain it will lose it (Matt 16:25)."[165]

We all suffer from these vices to one degree or another and the first dark night - the night of the senses - aims at purifying us of some of the bad habits that render us spiritually weak and vulnerable. But we're not finished yet. Where the night of the senses cut down the "weeds" of our imperfections, the night of the spirit must now take place to dig out the roots, which is why this latter night is so much more intense.

## *Fuel for the Journey*

This second night will not begin immediately after the first. God usually allows the person to enjoy its newfound freedom and satisfaction of spirit, sometimes for years before this final purification begins.

But once it does, it can be swift and intense. Purifications may come in the form of physical infirmities, spiritual afflictions and other humiliations meant to eradicate the last dregs of pride. Spiritual friends may suddenly turn on the person or a bad

---

[165] *Dark Night,* pg. 374-375

confessor or spiritual director may be allowed to cause interior confusion. Periods of aridity in prayer may become so acute that the soul feels as though God has completely abandoned it.

" . . . There are many things which assault her soul with an interior oppression so keenly felt and so intolerable that I do not know to what it can be compared save to the torment of those who suffer in hell, for in this spiritual test no consolation is possible."[166]

This is because the soul, who is intermittently receiving tremendous favors from God, now feels spiritually unclean and wretched.

"There is an impression of being rejected and abandoned by God. It appears that the person will never be worthy again and that the lofty blessings already received will never return."[167]

This experience can be so vivid, "that it seems to the soul that it sees hell and perdition open before it. These are the ones who go down into hell alive, since their purgation on earth is similar to that of purgatory."[168]

In fact, St. John of the Cross teaches that souls who undergo this purgation while on earth will be detained in purgatory only a short while, or not at all.

---

[166] *Interior Castle*, pg 131
[167] *Fire Within*, pg. 169
[168] *Dark Night*, pg. 339-40

Even though the soul might be experiencing days of rapturous prayer, it may be frequently punctuated by such a stark aridity the soul believes God may have decided to abandon it.

When this aridity strikes, "the soul feels as if it has never known God and never will know Him, and as if to hear His Majesty spoken of is like hearing of a person from a great distance away."[169]

This feeling is so pervasive that not even one's spiritual director can reassure them that all is not lost.

Thankfully, the worst of the deep pains of the second night are only felt at intervals and are mitigated by intervals of light and love.

Teresa aptly describes what it's like to be in the grips of this torment and intense aridity, saying that "there is no help for it but to wait upon the mercy of God, Who suddenly, at the most unlooked-for hour, with a single word, or on some chance occasion, lifts the whole of this burden from the soul, so that it seems as if it has never been clouded over, but is full of sunshine and far happier than it was before."[170]

## *Vital Virtue*

*Charity*

---

[169] Dark Night, 339-40

[170] Ibid, pg. 132

*At this point in our journey to God, we have come to that impasse where we must cease loving Him for our own's sake - because He's the source of our happiness and assistance. Even though loving God for all that He means to us is precious, it is still imperfect. Now it is time to love Him more perfectly.*

*Charity is the virtue that enables us to rise above loving God for our sakes in order to love Him for Who He is - for His goodness, beauty, wisdom and power. This is perfect love because it is pure love, that is, "love which takes complacence in the infinite good of God, and desires this good not for any personal advantage, but for God Himself, for His felicity, His glory," Father Gabriel teaches us.*

*"Charity elevates our love and makes us capable of really loving God as He loves Himself, although not with the same intensity."*

*For instance, there is a very pure and affectionate love of friendship among the three divine Persons by which each of them delights in the good and happiness of the others, and each desires the glory of the others.*

*"Charity makes us capable of loving God with this love of friendship, so as to love Him above all for Himself, for His glory and His happiness."*

*Even though none of us can add to the charity shared between the three divine Persons, "we can try with all our strength to please Him, to obtain for Him, if we may use the expression, the joy of seeing us correspond fully to His love; it urges us to seek His will, His interest, and His glory, before everything else, by renouncing our own will and personal interests," Fr. Gabriel writes.*

*This is how we achieve what St. Thomas Aquinas wrote: "Charity unites man's affection to God in such a way that he no longer lives for himself, but for God."*

## *Opportunities for Advancement*

What is needed to advance to the seventh mansion is to do what we are least inclined to do - "be fully accepting of this arduous, arid, trying pursuit of God."[171]

We cannot proceed without seeing the last of our perfections burned away. There can be no dirt left upon the windows of the soul. We have arrived at the summit of our earthly existence and are about to gaze upon what "eye has not seen nor ear heard".[172] We are about to receive what God reserves for those who truly love Him.

## *For Reflection*

1. How many hours a day do you spend watching TV, surfing the Internet, checking your phone, texting, etc.? Is this all necessary? What other circumstances make it

---

[171] *Fire Within*, pg 173
[172] Isaiah 64:3

difficult for you to find solitude in your life?

2. List the three reasons why the devil cannot mimic advanced experiences from God.

3. Yes, there's a "spiritual version" of the Seven Deadly Sins. Which ones can you spot in yourself? Ask the Holy Spirit to lend you the courage and generosity of heart to weed out these weaknesses and overcome them.

4. Have you ever experienced visions, either corporeal or imaginative? Why does St. John recommend that we ignore them? What are some of the dangers of hanging on to these visions and whatever messages they might have conveyed to us?

______________________________________________

______________________________________________

______________________________________________

______________________________________________

______________________________________________

______________________________________________

______________________________________________

# Chapter Seven

# THE SEVENTH MANSION

"You will think, sisters, that so much has been said about this spiritual road that there cannot possibly be any more to say. It would be a great mistake to think that; just as the greatness of God is without limit, even so are His works."[173]

So said St. Teresa of Avila to her nuns about this final transition from the sixth into the seventh mansion of the soul. She will struggle to explain what happens next in the journey because what the soul experiences is beyond the scope of human language.

" . . . In this mansion, everything is different. Our good God now desires to remove the scales from the eyes of the soul so that it may see and understand something of the favor which He is granting it, although He is doing this in a strange manner," she explains.

[173]Avila, Teresa, *Interior Castle*, translated and edited by E. Allison Peers (New York, NY, *Doubleday Books*, 1989), pg. 206

"It is brought into this mansion by means of an intellectual vision in which, by a representation of the truth in a particular way, the Most Holy Trinity reveals Itself, in all three Persons. First of all the spirit becomes enkindled and is illumined, as it were, by a cloud of the greatest brightness. It sees these three Persons, individually, and yet, by a wonderful kind of knowledge which is given to it, the soul realizes that most certainly and truly all these three Persons are one Substance and one Power and one Knowledge and one God alone, so that what we hold by faith the soul may be said to grasp by sight, although nothing is seen by the eyes, either of the body or of the soul. . . . Here all three Persons communicate Themselves to the soul and speak to the soul and explain to it those words which the Gospel attributes to the Lord - namely, that He and the Father and the Holy Spirit will come to dwell with the soul which loves Him and keeps His commandments."[174]

Teresa was brought into the seventh mansion just after receiving Communion one day from the hands of St. John of the Cross. He had broken the host in two in order to provide for another nun and because Teresa had once told him that she liked when the hosts were large, she thought he had done this to mortify her.

Deep inside, she heard the Lord speak. "Don't fear, daughter, for no one will be a party to separating you from Me." In that instant, the broken host no longer mattered.

---

[174] *Interior Castle,* pg. 209-210

"Then He appeared to me in an imaginative vision . . . and He gave me His right hand and said: 'Behold this nail; it is a sign you will be My bride from today on. Until now you have not merited this; from now on not only will you look after My honor as being the honor of your Creator, King and God, but you will look after it as My true bride. My honor is yours, and yours is mine'."[175]

Teresa's reaction to this grace beyond all graces was to shrink in humility.

"I asked the Lord either to raise me from my lowliness or not grant me such a favor; for it didn't seem to me my nature could bear it," she wrote. "Throughout the whole day I remained thus very absorbed. Afterward I felt great pain, and greater confusion and affliction at seeing I don't render any service in exchange for such amazing favors."

Her reaction was much like that of Peter when, after a disappointing night of fishing, set out to fish once again at the Lord's command and caught so many his nets were breaking. He was so astonished that he fell at the Lord's feet and said, "Depart from me Lord, for I am a sinful man."[176]

Teresa was quickly to learn that her marriage to the Lord was not a passing favor but would become her permanent state of being. Each day thereafter she would

---

[175] Kavanaugh, Kieran OCD, Rodriquez, Otilio, OCD, *The Collected Works of Teresa of Avila, Volume One, Spiritual Testimonies* (Washington, DC, ICS Publications) No. 31, pg. 402
[176] Luke 5:8

awake to amazement when realizing that this unique new awareness of the indwelling Trinity was still there.

As she describes, she was able to quite clearly perceive Them in the interior of her heart, "in the most interior place of all and in its greatest depths." Some days this perception would be more clear than others, but after the occasion of her marriage to the Lord, it remained with her always.

Teresa described this awareness as being in a bright room with very many people when suddenly the lights are turned off.

"The light by which they can be seen has been taken away, and, until it comes back, we shall be unable to see them, yet we are none the less aware that they are there."[177]

We might be tempted to think that a person who has received such a favor is so absorbed in God that she is capable of nothing else, but this is far from the case.

"In all that belongs to the service of God, she is more alert than before; and when not otherwise occupied, she rests in that happy companionship,"[178] Teresa writes.

Sometimes called "dual awareness and operation", this trait enables individuals to attend to the indwelling Trinity while carrying on their ordinary affairs.

---

[177] *Interior Castle*, pg 211
[178] Ibid, pg. 210

This continual presence is all part of the Lord's plan for those who have proven their love for Him. Speaking to another one of His brides, St. Catherine of Siena, He referred to this journey from intermittent to permanent union as a "loving game":

"I told you how I go away from others (in feeling only, not in grace) and then return. I do not act thus with these most perfect ones who have attained great perfection, and are completely dead to every selfish impulse. No, I am always at rest and in their souls both by grace and by feeling. In other words, they can join their spirits with me in loving affection whenever they will."

Once in this state, nothing can separate the soul from God and every time and place for them is a time and place of prayer.

"They have been made one with me and I with them. I will never withdraw from their feelings. No, their spirits always feel my presence within them, whereas of the others I . . . come and go . . . and I do this to bring them to perfection. When they reach perfection I relieve them of this lover's game of going and coming back. I call it a 'lover's game' because I go away for love and I come back for love . . ."[179]

So enduring is this state that no matter how numerous were Teresa's trials and business worries, the essential part of her soul was permanently fixed in this placid

---

[179] Quoted in Martin, Ralph, *The Fulfillment of All Desire* (Steubenville, OH, *Emmaus Road Publishing*, 2006) pg. 404

dwelling place. In fact, she once described herself as feeling divided because her soul remained in perfect peace even while life was erupting as usual all around her. Sometimes she would even grumble that her soul was "doing nothing but enjoying itself" while she was left with all the trials of life.

This description should dismiss any notion that the person who reaches the seventh mansion is somehow marginal or strange. Rather, this individual is more fully engaged in life than any of us.

St. Teresa once described herself as being "better in every way" after this union took place.

The person who has achieved spiritual marriage has certain distinctive traits. One of them is complete self-forgetfulness.

"There is a self-forgetfulness which is so complete that it really seems as though the soul no longer exists because it is such that she has neither knowledge nor remembrance that there is either heaven or life or honor for her, so entirely is she employed in seeking the honor of God," the saint describes.[180]

The second effect upon the person is to instill within it a great desire to suffer, "but this is not of such a kind as to disturb the soul, as it did previously. So extreme is her longing for the will of God to be done in her that whatever His Majesty does she considers to be for the

---

[180] Interior Castle, pg. 219

best: if He wills that she should suffer, well and good; if not, she does not worry herself to death as she did before."[181]

Souls who reach this mansion shift from wanting to die to enjoy the Lord more fully to wanting to live a long time so that they might bring souls to God.

Persecution no longer frightens them. Instead, persecutions inspire "a great interior joy . . . . They bear no enmity to those who ill-treat them, or desire to do so. Indeed, they conceive a special love for them, so that, if they see them in some trouble, they are deeply grieved and would do anything possible to relieve them.; they love to comment them to God and they would rejoice at not being given some of the favors which His Majesty bestows upon them if their enemies might have been instead and thus be prevented from offending Our Lord."[182]

Gone are all of those interior aridities and trials they once suffered. Instead, they feel a tender love for Him, so much so that they would prefer to do nothing as much as praising Him and otherwise attending to Him.

Even the raptures and flights of spirit cease, except for rare occasions.

Should the soul "wander off" in her attention, "the Lord Himself awakens it . . . so that it sees quite clearly

---

[181] Ibid, pg. 220
[182] Ibid

that this impulse, or whatever it is called, proceeds from the interior of the soul . . . "[183]

The Lord strengthens His bride from the inside out.

"Previously, the poor little butterfly was always so worried that everything frightened her and made her fly away. But it is not so now, whether because she has found her rest, or because the soul has seen so much in this Mansion that it can be frightened at nothing . . . . (T)hey lose the great weakness which was such a trial to them and of which previously they could not rid themselves."[184]

Most of all, this soul is now perfected in love which brings about "a freedom from self-concern and fear of what others will think that enables one to act with a daring and determination in obedience to God's will and His interests."[185]

No matter what, this soul now has the fortitude to always act in the service of love, regardless of the cost.

"The soul easily extracts the sweetness of love from all the things that happen to her; that is, she loves God in them," writes St. John of the Cross.

"Thus everything leads her to love. And being informed and fortified as she is with love, she neither feels nor tastes nor knows the things that happen to her, whether delightful or bitter, since as we said the soul

---

[183] Ibid, pg. 222

[184] Ibid, pg. 224

[185] *The Fulfillment of All Desire*, pg. 386

knows nothing else but love . . . God makes use of nothing other than love."[186]

This soul now has a great sensitivity to others and a keen ability to reach out them in their need. Like St. Paul advises, she becomes all things to all people with a total lack of self-concern.

"Although I am free in regard to all, I have made myself a slave to all so as to win over as many as possible. To the Jews I became as a Jew, in order to win Jews. To those under the law I became as one under the law (though not being myself under the law) that I might win those under the law. To those outside the law I became as one outside the law (not being outside the law of God but under the law of Christ) that I might win those outside the law. To the weak I became weak, that I might win the weak. I have become all things to all people, that by all means I might save some. I do it all for the sake of the gospel, that I may share with them in its blessings."[187]

Only the person perfected in love can behave in such a manner.

Love . . . at the beginning, at the middle, and at the end of the journey, is the substance of true holiness and the fruit of genuine union with God.

---

[186] *The Fulfillment of All Desire*, pg 387
[187] 1 Corinthians 19:22

True sanctity has nothing to do with kneeling in prayer all day and staring at the heavens. It's all about action which is fueled by the fire of love.

Consequently, this stage of union with God has a dramatic impact on the devil. As St. John of the Cross explains, the devil is actually afraid of these souls.

"In this state the soul is so protected and strong in each of the virtues and in all of them together . . . that the devils not only fear to attack her but do not even venture to appear before her. For they become greatly frightened on seeing her so exalted, courageous, and bold, with the perfect virtues in the bed of her Beloved. When she is united with God in transformation they fear her as much as they do Him, and they dare not even look at her. The devil has an extraordinary fear of the perfect soul."[188]

These are just some of the good effects experienced by a soul who has persevered in the journey and achieved the great crown that awaits it in the seventh mansion.

"Here to this sounded hart are given waters in abundance. Here the soul delights in the tabernacle of God. Here the dove sent out by Noah to see if the storm is over finds the olive branch - the sign that it has discovered firm ground amidst the waters and storms of this world."[189]

---

[188] *The Fulfillment of All Desire*, pg. 401
[189] *Interior Castle*, pg. 224

# *Conclusion*

After reading about such a fantastic journey, one can't help but ask whether ordinary people like us have any chance at all of getting this far. The answer is a resounding "yes!"

Remember, the Lord always chooses the person we least expect - you!

The saints didn't make it to the seventh mansion because they were so holy. They made it because they were humble enough to admit they weren't. Only then could they fully appreciate the tremendous gift given to them at the moment of their baptism - the Holy Spirit, the Sanctifier, the One who comes with all the power of the universe at His disposal.

We are all little silkworms, weak and incapable and full of faults, and the price we pay to make this fantastic mystical journey is complete death-to-self, something our human nature will fight every step of the way.

But there are no short cuts. All must travel by way of the authentic Gospel. We must decrease and He must increase. This is the dying process that will reveal to us the great secret of the saints - to rely on God alone.

When this vital lesson is learned, the little silkworm can begin the long descent into its silken tomb, from which only God can resurrect a beautiful new butterfly.

## *For Reflection*

1. Now that you have reached the end of this incredible journey, what kind of emotions does it inspire with you? Awe? Wonder? Love? If you could sum up this journey in one word, what would it be?

______________________________________________

______________________________________________

______________________________________________

______________________________________________

______________________________________________

______________________________________________

2. The devil wants nothing more than to convince us that we'll never make it to the seventh mansion. How will you go about proving him wrong?

______________________________________________

______________________________________________

______________________________________________

______________________________________________

______________________________________________

______________________________________________

3. How has your opinion about holiness and sanctity changed as a result of this journey?

______________________________________________

______________________________________________

______________________________________________

______________________________________________

______________________________________________

______________________________________________

# *NOTES*

# *NOTES*

# *NOTES*

## *About Live Catholic*

The mission of the Catholic Life Institute is now being carried out by Live Catholic!

We are a lay-run apostolate founded by Secular Discalced Carmelites from various communities throughout the United States who are devoted to infusing the world with the truth of the Catholic mystical tradition as revealed by the Carmelite saints and Doctors of the Church.

Our aim is to make the teachings of St. Teresa of Avila, St. John of the Cross, St. Therese of Lisieux, and other Carmelite saints more accessible and understandable to the faithful. We offer courses explaining St. Teresa's four stages of prayer and the seven mansions of the soul, as well as St. Therese's Little Way of Spiritual Childhood. Our courses, workshops and conferences also include instruction on spiritual warfare, discernment, how to acquire Peace of Soul, and a variety of other topics. Courses and workshops are taught in both cohort-based (live instruction) and self-paced learning (provided via Teachables). In addition, these learning materials are offered on-demand, meaning parishes and other small groups can request a course/workshop to be taught on the day/time of their choosing.

All of our courses have an imprimatur from the Archdiocese of Philadelphia and are faithful to the Magisterium and free of any New Age components.

For more information visit www.livecatholic.org or contact us at info@livecatholic.org.

Made in the USA
Monee, IL
06 February 2024

53049828R00095